About the Author

Dennis Zines has been playing competitive bridge mainly from Sydney, Australia since circa 1968 and has had mediocre success most of the time, but very occasionally punctuated with regional or national success. This qualifies him as an average player, but one who is willing to record and write about the stories that would otherwise disappear in the shuffling of the cards.

In this collection he relates what happened on a number of deals that piqued his interest. No doubt you will recognise similar circumstances and outcomes and hopefully will enjoy the journey.

This is not an educational book but potentially one where you can pick it up at any time for a slight bridge diversion from whatever else that you were doing that you really didn't want to do.

To aspiring bridge players

DENNIS ZINES

EVERYDAY BRIDGE
ADVENTURES

AUSTIN MACAULEY
PUBLISHERS LTD.

A CIP catalogue record for this title is available from the British Library.

ISBN 9781785541322 (Paperback)
ISBN 9781785541339 (Hardback)

www.austinmacauley.com

First Published (2015)
Austin Macauley Publishers Ltd.
25 Canada Square
Canary Wharf
London
E14 5LQ

Printed and bound in Great Britain

Acknowledgments

Thanks to:

Tina Zines for her skill and patience in editing the text and correcting errors.

Max Mendez of Mendez Branding for providing the amazing illustrations.

Matthew Thompson and Ron Klinger for advice on preparing the text.

INTRODUCTION

Thoughts in writing this book

I am now retired and am playing a little more bridge than before although not with the fervour of an earlier era. I thought about doing something useful with my extra time – instead I am collecting odd bridge hands and compiling them into this book.

Most bridge books are written by erudite authors who set out to instruct and dazzle their readers. Not so this volume. Instead I am setting out to record the ups and downs of the everyday punter who aspires yet only sometimes achieves, but who observes the ebb and flow and glimpses what might have been.

I have always puzzled about the strangeness of Bridge where you can play against the best just by paying your entry money. And today you can even play *with* the best just by paying their fee (i.e. hire a pro).

In either case you can do well at any one time (usually over a very short period), which is not what you would expect when playing other games. For example, do you really think you could win a game at tennis – let alone a set – from the Joker (Novak Djokovic)? Or at golf outdrive the Tiger (Woods)? Or even hit a six from any first grade bowler?

The stories and reported hands in this book are genuine and sometimes feature really fine exponents of the game (alas usually my opponents) plus an on-the-spot reporter (me) who has tried playing the game for many years and who is not scared to keep on trying for those moments of fame that do occur, even if a little too rarely these days.

I also like to report on things that interest me and I hope the reader of this chronicle also enjoys the drolleries and injustices that are the regular experiences of the average player.

Since Bridge is a beautiful game filled with skill, knowledge, flair, psychology and luck (you can but only rarely choose the percentages of each) together with seemingly boundless possibilities and entertaining (or devastating) outcomes, there is always a "story".

So, apart from this being a time-filler for me, I think that as in "The Naked City" (only the elderly will recall the TV series I am referring to), there are thousands of stories out there and these are but a few. I enjoy writing about them and I hope that you will enjoy reading them. You may not improve your bridge by reading this book, but I do hope you enjoy its content and recognise that even the mediocre can have a short time in the sun while more often suffering the slings and arrows of outrageous fortune. It also shows how things just turn up at the table that are worth recording and enjoying at leisure.

The chapters are loosely themed for amusement. And so...

Contents

1   Chapter 1 – Who said Bridge is Fair?

Bridge has its random side and is shockingly unconcerned with fairness.

Here is a typical example of randomness. You are West as dealer and the bidding goes:

WEST	NORTH	EAST	SOUTH
Pass	Pass	2♣ (1)	2♥
Pass	4♥	All Pass	

1. 11-16 hcp and six clubs.

2. You hold and need to lead from:

♠106532

♥J10

♦QJ83

♣Q7

Did you lead partner's club suit like me and suffer -620? The full hand:

Dealer West – All Vulnerable

♠Q94
♥K98742
♦1097
♣K

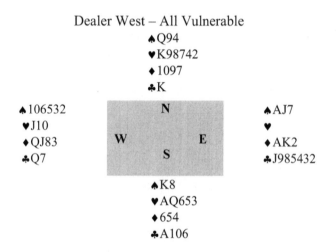

```
♠106532              N              ♠AJ7
♥J10                                ♥
♦QJ83         W           E         ♦AK2
♣Q7                 S              ♣J985432

                 ♠K8
                 ♥AQ653
                 ♦654
                 ♣A106
```

Most pairs were in 4♥ all declared from North (who no doubt opened with a weak two bid) allowing a diamond lead. This is just typical of playing against different systems – some you win, some you lose.

There is not a lot to learn from this hand apart from the ugly realisation that it's not always your fault.

Of course, there is still a sour taste in your mouth at the time.

This is definitely a curious and uncommon deal.

Dealer East – North-South Vulnerable

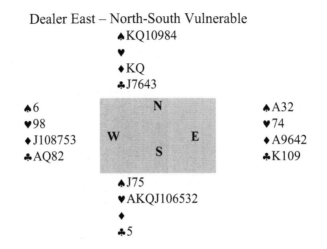

Not often you hold a solid nine-bagger. Anyway, East opens 1♦ and South (me) prosaically bids 4♥. West makes a great bid of 5♦ and it returns to me.

After due deliberation, I pass and theoretically win the war with 5♦ going one down (a positive score) while even 4♥ can go one down with a spade lead and ruff followed by the underlead of the ♣A to get another ruff. (Has a thoughtful East returned ♠2 knowing ♦A won't fly? Not so easy from West's view if East is 4-4 in the minors).

However at the table bridge theory is for the birds. Three declarers are allowed to make ten to twelve tricks in hearts on the ♠6 lead!!! West probably led a diamond at trick three instead of cashing the ♣A or underleading it.

Passing at least is not as bad as bidding 5♥ (assuming any reasonable defence).

This next deal was originally reported in *Australian Bridge* in June 1977 but is reproduced here with some further insight. The bidding was exuberant from both North and South and was justified only by the result.

Dealer South – Nil Vulnerable

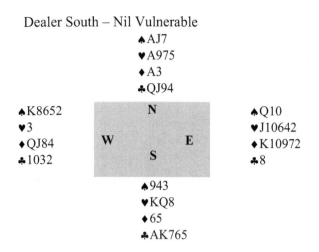

♠ AJ7
♥ A975
♦ A3
♣ QJ94

♠ K8652
♥ 3
♦ QJ84
♣ 1032

♠ Q10
♥ J10642
♦ K10972
♣ 8

♠ 943
♥ KQ8
♦ 65
♣ AK765

The bidding went as follows:

WEST	NORTH	EAST	SOUTH
		Pass	1NT (1)
Pass	2♦ (2)	Pass	3♣ (3)
Pass	6♣ (4)	All Pass	

1. Playing 13-15 hcp range – assume South (me) couldn't count to 13
2. Game-forcing Stayman
3. 5-card club suit, no 4-card major
4. Slam try!

The initial view of dummy did not fill me with delight, but West's lead of the ♥3 assisted the line of play.

The ♥5 drew the ♥10 and the ♥Q. Three rounds of trumps were drawn ending in dummy and East's discards convinced me that West had led a singleton so I then finessed the ♥8, cashed the ♥K and entered dummy with the ♠A. The ♥A allowed a diamond discard followed by a diamond ruff.

Having eliminated three suits, I then led a spade towards the jack, playing for honour doubleton with East, and was duly rewarded.

The slam could always be made on any lead in the same way, but in practice declarer wouldn't take this line. The helpful lead of the singleton heart basically forced me to take the right line, demonstrating how important it is to get the defenders' help and how fickle is your bridge fate.

On another day, the singleton lead would be the only way to beat the slam.

The following two deals were published in *Australian Bridge* in February 1979 and actually occurred on one of my better nights at the club. My partner at the time was Peter Wood.

My partner's excursions into fantasy during his bidding had progressed beyond legendary status and at the time of these hands were accepted as commonplace.

From time to time I tried to redirect his undoubted talents to more conventional ends but rarely did I prevail. Instead, witness this effort where I as North blatantly tried to mimic his follies by bidding to what all accounts should have been a contract doomed to ignominy.

Dealer East – All Vulnerable

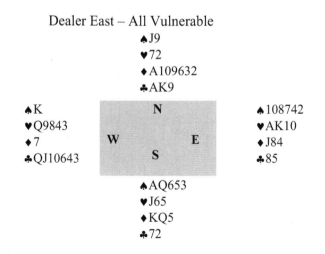

```
                  ♠ J9
                  ♥ 72
                  ♦ A109632
                  ♣ AK9
   ♠ K              N              ♠ 108742
   ♥ Q9843                         ♥ AK10
   ♦ 7          W       E          ♦ J84
   ♣ QJ10643        S              ♣ 85
                  ♠ AQ653
                  ♥ J65
                  ♦ KQ5
                  ♣ 72
```

The bidding went as follows:

WEST	NORTH	EAST	SOUTH
		Pass	1♠
1NT	Double	Pass	Pass
2♣	3♣	Pass	3♦
Pass	4♦	Pass	4♠
Pass	4NT	Pass	5♦
Pass	6♦	Double	All Pass

The bidding probably left everyone confused. The 1♠ bid is normal but the 1NT conventionally showed 5-11 points and 0-1 spade.

Determined not to be put off by such a peevish interpose, I carried the bidding to the slam level at which stage East decided that enough could be a feast. East's double caused not a little discomfiture for West and finally the ♠K hit the deck with the exclamation, 'I thought the double called for an unusual lead'.

An unusual lead indeed! My partner won the ♠A, cashed the ♦K and then the ♠J followed by ♣A, ♣K and a club ruff (East not ruffing – which wouldn't have helped). The ♦Q drew the second trump and then the ♠Q was cashed for a heart discard followed by a spade ruff, ♦A and a heart conceded, making twelve tricks for the contract.

Well the opponents left squabbling and while my partner gleefully calculated the score to be + 1540, I sat there in trepidation, fearful of perhaps being congratulated on my bold sequence. I had scarce recovered from self-diagnosed delusions of grandeur (or at least a small grandeur) when the following little gem shone forth:

Dealer West – North-South Vulnerable

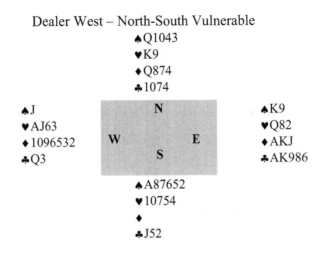

♠Q1043
♥K9
♦Q874
♣1074

♠J
♥AJ63
♦1096532
♣Q3

♠K9
♥Q82
♦AKJ
♣AK986

♠A87652
♥10754
♦
♣J52

After two passes, East opened a non-vulnerable 1♣ and partner threw in a vulnerable 1♠ overcall. West bid 2♥ and I innocently raised the ante to 2♠ (whereas 3♠ was probably the right bid, although perhaps not in 1979). A 4♥ bid from East drew an equally firm 4♠ from partner which in turn was even more firmly doubled by East (with some justification, one would feel, glancing at her modest collection).

WEST	NORTH	EAST	SOUTH
Pass	Pass	1♣	1♠
2♥	2♠	4♥	4♠
Pass	Pass	Double	All Pass

West led the ♥A and as I wondered if the blood preserved so neatly at the earlier table was to be shed here, I shouldn't have worried.

West rightly switched to the ♣Q and a second club, but East dreaming of large numbers, had had a brainwave. She started her long term plan by laying down the ♦K, intending no doubt to put her partner in with a club ruff for a further diamond through dummy.

Her efforts came to nought, as did her further tricks. Partner not only pinned the king and jack of spades, but also ruffed out the ♦A so as to discard the losing club on the ♦Q, ending up with the contract and +790.

I decided then and there that bidding reform was not the answer.

However, I do have a little sympathy with the parting comment of the last unfortunate pair. "Simply outrageous!" really covers the situation quite nicely, I think.

On the next deal I had several opportunities to go wrong and took them all for the worst score in the field.

Dealer North– East-West Vulnerable

♠752
♥AQ32
♦KQ4
♣K76

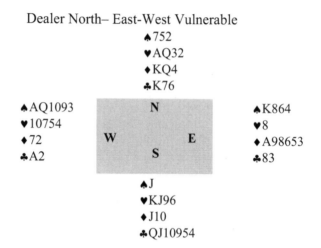

♠AQ1093   ♠K864
♥10754   ♥8
♦72   ♦A98653
♣A2   ♣83

♠J
♥KJ96
♦J10
♣QJ10954

The bidding:

WEST	NORTH	EAST	SOUTH
	1♣	Pass	1♥
1♠	2♥	3♥(1)	4♥(2)
Pass	Pass	4♠(3)	Pass
Pass	Double (4)	Pass	Pass (5)

1.   East showed a heart shortage (0-1) and invitational values.
2.   There is no doubt that West would have quit at 3♠ as evidenced by the pass of 4♥. So in making the 4♥ bid, South should have known what to do after the expected 4♠. South's values are soft and offer marginal defence.

3.   He made me do it.
4.   Obligatory since North-South had freely bid to game
5.   I shouldn't have bid 4♥ and now I don't know what to do.
Hope partner understands.

So, we scored minus 790 instead of minus 170 (their playing 3♠) or
minus 300 (in 5♥ doubled). East-West did well, but they needed help.
Most of the other East-West players allowed 4♥ to play and make. In
retrospect, we were destined to do badly, but the bad choices
maximised the damage.

This time blind, groping Justice had unerringly found her mark.

The following two deals are paired under the title "Missing Aces".
Generally speaking Aces win tricks, but it's not always so.

The first exhibit is as follows:

Dealer South– Nil Vulnerable

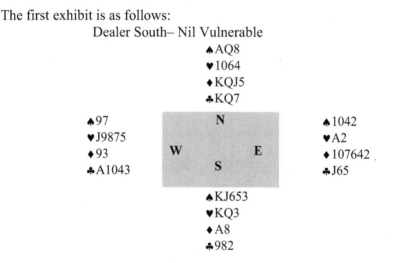

```
                    ♠AQ8
                    ♥1064
                    ♦KQJ5
                    ♣KQ7
    ♠97               N            ♠1042
    ♥J9875                         ♥A2
    ♦93          W       E         ♦107642
    ♣A1043           S             ♣J65
                    ♠KJ653
                    ♥KQ3
                    ♦A8
                    ♣982
```

North-South bid to 6♠ with many first- and second-round cue bids, but
without counting their Key Cards.

A simple heart lead would have promptly shown the deficiencies of this
approach, but I led a trump won by South. South thought a long time
before leading a club from hand.

This was the moment of truth. I ducked to see what would happen and was horrified at the outcome. The ♣Q won, a second trump was played and four diamonds saw the clubs in the South hand disappear.

A heart followed and as you can see, the slam made and the declarer purred while partner fumed. I didn't feel so good.

The related hand was in a Pairs event.

Dealer South– East-West Vulnerable

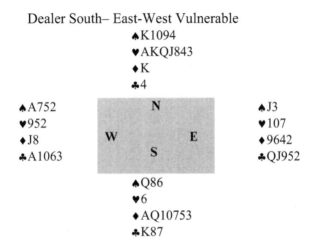

                    ♠K1094
                    ♥AKQJ843
                    ♦K
                    ♣4

♠A752   N   ♠J3
♥952   ♥107
♦J8   W   E   ♦9642
♣A1063   S   ♣QJ952

                    ♠Q86
                    ♥6
                    ♦AQ10753
                    ♣K87

The bidding from East-West was slow, tortuous and full of doubt.

WEST	NORTH	EAST	SOUTH
			1♦
Pass	1♥	Pass	2♦
Pass	2♠	Pass	2NT
Pass	3♥	Pass	3♠
Pass	4NT	Pass	5♦
Pass	5♥	Pass	5♠
Pass	5NT	All Pass	

South opened 1♦ and rebid 2♦ after hearing 1♥ from North. North bid 2♠ game forcing and South fortuitously bid 2NT at this point.

Thereafter North repeated his hearts with South reasonably gave Spade preference at this time. North Blackwooded in Spades, realised two

Keycards were missing and tried to sign off in 5♥, but South didn't get the gag, so once again gave preference back to spades.

North in desperation and hope returned to 5NT.
As West on lead, I could have tabled my two aces to prevent any further delays, but hopefully led a club.

Dummy was then on view to all, including my partner, who should now know I have two aces.

South won the ♣K and started to play many hearts. Partner, who had forgotten the bidding or just wanted to get rid of those pesky diamonds, threw his "useless" diamonds.

Not long after, declarer claimed thirteen tricks without losing any club or spade aces.

We were set for 4% with them in 5NT (cold for eleven tricks) but received 0%, so in real terms the loss was trivial, but the blood pressure rise was certainly life threatening and very damaging for partnership harmony.

Traditional theory says that holding aces is a good thing, but appearances can be deceiving.

The next deal verges on the surreal.

There should be a moral here or at least some more enterprise by East-West.

South opened a weak NT and probably regretted it. North (me) had a dose of unreality and bid 3NT.

WEST	NORTH	EAST	SOUTH
			1NT
Pass	3NT	All Pass	

Dealer South – All Vulnerable

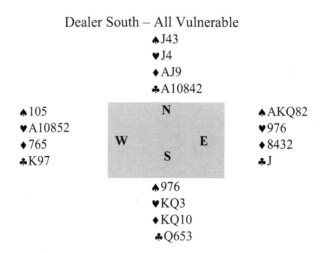

```
                    ♠ J43
                    ♥ J4
                    ♦ AJ9
                    ♣ A10842
♠ 105                   N                   ♠ AKQ82
♥ A10852                                    ♥ 976
♦ 765            W           E              ♦ 8432
♣ K97                   S                   ♣ J
                    ♠ 976
                    ♥ KQ3
                    ♦ KQ10
                    ♣ Q653
```

East should have doubled in pique for a spade lead but didn't. South passed and West led the ♥ 5.

Upon seeing dummy, South called triple 0, but while he was waiting for the ambulance won the ♥ Q and led the ♣ Q playing for the miracle lie and was duly rewarded (?) with nine tricks.

North-South maybe didn't really get their just deserts, but perhaps East-West did. On balance, not really so unfair?

The following deal demonstrates that Science is overrated and pre-emption is better (although not at our team mates' table).

Dealer West– East-West Vulnerable

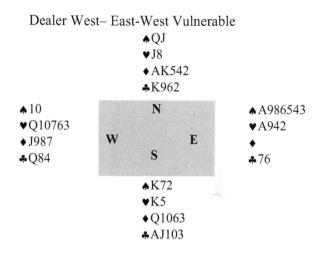

♠QJ
♥J8
♦AK542
♣K962

♠10
♥Q10763
♦J987
♣Q84

♠A986543
♥A942
♦
♣76

♠K72
♥K5
♦Q1063
♣AJ103

At our table, my partner North opened 1♦ playing Precision showing 11-16hcp and at least two diamonds. East overcalled 1♠ and I as South contemplated 3NT. Looking deeper, I thought that if partner had the ♠Q, then 3NT would be better by him, so I bid 2♠.

North bid 3♣ (not understanding my desire for him to bid NT) and believe it or not, East bid 3♥ which West raised to 4♥.

WEST	NORTH	EAST	SOUTH
Pass	1♦	1♠	2♠
Pass	3♣	3♥	3NT
4♥	Pass	Pass	Double
All Pass			

Of course, I had to double and good fortune saw me hold it to ten tricks only for -790.

Conversely, my team mates overcalled 3♠, forcing South to bid 3NT. Naturally West led a spade eschewing the winning heart lead and in the ensuing confusion South ended up with only nine tricks for plus 400 - completing the perfect board (for the opposition).

WEST	NORTH	EAST	SOUTH
Pass	1♦	3♠	3NT
All Pass			

Recently the following deal turned up which strongly reminded me of the previous deal.

Dealer South – Nil Vulnerable

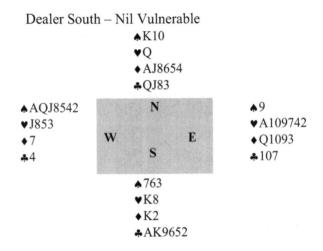

```
                    ♠K10
                    ♥Q
                    ♦AJ8654
                    ♣QJ83
  ♠AQJ8542        N              ♠9
  ♥J853                          ♥A109742
  ♦7         W         E         ♦Q1093
  ♣4              S              ♣107
                    ♠763
                    ♥K8
                    ♦K2
                    ♣AK9652
```

At my table South (my partner) opened 1♣ and West bid 3♠. After a lot of consideration, I emerged with the wrong bid of 5♣. This contract went one down after the ♠A followed by a ruff and the ♥A.

As you can see, nine tricks in 3NT is untouchable from either North or South and in retrospect is the bid I should have made. This is what occurred at the other table so we lost heavily.

However, both Wests missed genuine opportunities for glory.

Firstly, they could have bid 4♠ directly preventing 3NT by North-South. This would have resulted in being either one down or pushing North-South to the losing 5♣ contract. Either is better than 3NT making by North-South.

Secondly, they had a free kick which could have turned to gold. This is how I think the bidding should have gone.

WEST	NORTH	EAST	SOUTH
			1♣
3♠	3NT	Pass	Pass
4♥			

You may be shocked to see me recommending the 4♥ bid, but consider the following:

West did not make a Michaels overcall of the opening 1♣ bid but did bid 3♠ showing seven in that suit. Thus West is shapely and weak and the heart suit is clearly a secondary suit. The heart bid will normally be converted to 4♠ rectifying the previous underbid of 3♠ and would be saving against the 3NT contract.

In this case, East will happily pass and unless North-South now themselves save in 5♣, then they will turn out to be the biggest loser.

You may think I am fantasising, but a little imagination goes a long way in shapely hands.

If I had been in the West seat, perhaps my memories of the previous hand would have allowed the above to actually come to pass?

Speaking of pre-empts, on the following deal I considered opening 4♠, but instead went for the scientific 1♠.

Dealer South – North-South Vulnerable

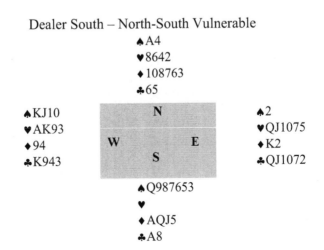

```
                    ♠A4
                    ♥8642
                    ♦108763
                    ♣65
    ♠KJ10               N            ♠2
    ♥AK93                            ♥QJ1075
    ♦94          W          E       ♦K2
    ♣K943               S            ♣QJ1072
                    ♠Q987653
                    ♥
                    ♦AQJ5
                    ♣A8
```

WEST	NORTH	EAST	SOUTH
			1♠
Double	Pass	2♥	2♠
3♥	Pass	Pass	3♠
Pass	Pass	4♥	All Pass

Although I kept bidding spades vulnerable (three times) to the three level, partner couldn't see his way to the four level, so we successfully defeated 4♥ by West for plus 50.

When I found out that North had five diamonds, I feared the worst which naturally came to pass.

At the other table, they successfully held 4♠ doubled to ten tricks (-790).

So, I should pre-empt more often, but my team mates shouldn't (at least on these boards).
Some days, it doesn't pay to get out of bed, let alone try to do well at a bridge tournament.

As you will see on this deal, our opponents were treated badly by a man who can't even count (me) let alone know what the bidding means. I was South playing with a substitute and trying to remember certain of her preferences.

After East passed, I opened 1NT (15-17). As you can see from the deal below, thirteen is well short of the required amount for this bid. The bidding proceeded as shown below.

WEST	NORTH	EAST	SOUTH
		Pass	1NT (1)
2♣ (2)	Double (3)	Pass	Pass (4)
2♦ (5)	Double (6)	3♦ (7)	3♥ (8)
All Pass			

1. As explained above
2. Single-suited take-out
3. Discussed as showing clubs, but I forgot and thought it said I would

have bid 2♣ asking about majors
4. I passed in fright as I had now re-counted my actual points
5. West honestly showed his suit
6. Showing values but I still thought it was take-out for the majors
7. Upping the ante
8. Showing hearts but not denying spades.

West led the ♣Q, an obvious singleton.

Dealer East – North-South Vulnerable

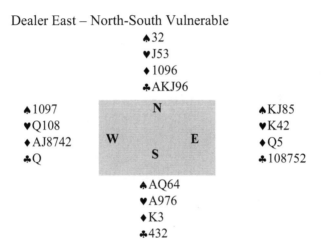

                    ♠32
                    ♥J53
                    ♦1096
                    ♣AKJ96
♠1097   ♠KJ85
♥Q108   ♥K42
♦AJ8742   ♦Q5
♣Q   ♣108752
                    ♠AQ64
                    ♥A976
                    ♦K3
                    ♣432

The sight of dummy jogged my memory as to partner's bidding
intentions and I settled down to minimise the damage. I won the club in
dummy and took the spade finesse, cashed the spade ace and took a
spade ruff. I now led the ♥5 which drew the ♥2, ♥6 and ♥8.

West now on lead was out of spades and wanted to avoid leading
diamonds so had to lead a trump (the queen is helpful to East and is
also the successful defence).

Unfortunately he led the ten which then saw the jack from dummy and
the king from East (he should have ducked locking me in dummy). I
won ace and again threw West in with the ♥Q. He resignedly led ace
and another diamond (rectifying the count) after which time I was able
to squeeze East in spades and clubs.

A true comedy of errors with me as the primary culprit finishing with the Cheshire cat grin and East-West having much discussion.

Justice again took a holiday.

PS – If I double 3♦ we can get 300 on accurate defence, but that wouldn't have been as satisfying an outcome.
This deal features multiple endplays, whether played by North or East, and two tales of woe.

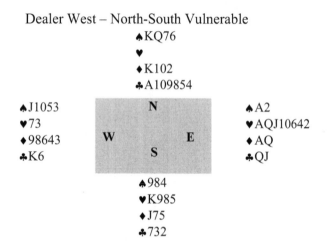

Dealer West – North-South Vulnerable

```
                 ♠KQ76
                 ♥
                 ♦K102
                 ♣A109854
♠J1053                              ♠A2
♥73          N                     ♥AQJ10642
♦98643    W       E                ♦AQ
♣K6          S                     ♣QJ
                 ♠984
                 ♥K985
                 ♦J75
                 ♣732
```

At our table after a pass from me as West, North opens 1♣. My partner as East bids 4♥ and after two passes, North doubles (presumably for take-out) but all pass.

WEST	NORTH	EAST	SOUTH
Pass	1♣	4♥	Pass
Pass	Double	All Pass	

So far so good since my partner is in a makeable contract. If South leads a spade, say the nine, then West and North cover and East wins the ace and follows up by playing clubs. North must duck round one to avoid giving East an easy entry to finesse diamonds, but after winning the second club is endplayed. So, theoretically we are plus 590.

18

At our team mates' table (them being North-South), the initial bidding is the same but North bids 4♠ at her second turn which is doubled by East.

What should happen now is that South corrects to 5♣ and my team is minus 500 in 5♣X. A theoretical pick-up of 90. Whoopee!

Against the 5♣X contract, East is regularly endplayed from trick one. Even though a club lead may allow West to get in for a diamond lead, the defence can only get four tricks.

WEST	NORTH	EAST	SOUTH
Pass	1♣	4♥	Pass
Pass	4♠	Double	5♣
Double	All Pass		

Meanwhile, let's get back to the real world. The defence against East's 4♥ at my table is simplistic. The first club is taken and East gets an early entry to dummy for the diamond finesse. Spurning the obvious and successful line, my former partner (not just this hand) goes one off for minus 100.

At the other table, for some inexplicable reason, North is left in 4♠X resulting in minus 1400 for a net loss of 1500. Two promising gold starts are converted into dross and another case of what might have been. I am not so sure I would have bid again on the North cards vulnerable after partner had already passed, but hey!

Same teams event with same team mates and same match.

At our table after a pass from North, my partner East opens 1♥. South overcalls 2♣ and I as West bid a non-forcing 2♦ which North doubles.

WEST	NORTH	EAST	SOUTH
		1♥	2♣
2♦	Double	All Pass	

19

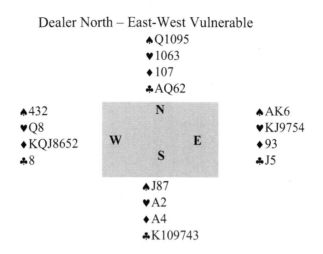

♠Q1095
♥1063
♦107
♣AQ62

♠432　　　　　　　　　　　♠AK6
♥Q8　　　　　　　　　　　♥KJ9754
♦KQJ8652　　　　　　　　♦93
♣8　　　　　　　　　　　　♣J5

♠J87
♥A2
♦A4
♣K109743

South passes stating in no uncertain terms that he doesn't understand North's bid and North shouldn't make bids that he doesn't understand since he will always pass when this happens.

I wrap up nine tricks (they play spades twice) for plus 380. I am smiling since I have a good score and they are arguing. We are also well up in the match at this stage.

I didn't allow for the other table. After a murky auction, East reaches 4♥. Good, you say, since it can go off two, doubled or not.

Partners don't see it that way and take the sac in 5♣X for minus 300.

Time for a new partner and new team mates?

The bridge table is not a place for sleeping, but that didn't stop me.

As South, I held:

♠32
♥J963
♦Q75
♣AJ42

WEST	NORTH	EAST	SOUTH
		Pass	Pass
Pass	1♦	Pass	1♥
Pass	3♣	Pass	5♣
Pass	5♥	All Pass	

After three passes, partner (North) opened 1♦ and I replied 1♥. So far so good. Partner then bid 3♣ and in a flash I bid 5♣! Partner bid 5♥ and it was then that I awoke from my reverie. Partner's club bid was a mini-splinter showing club shortage, heart support and about 15-17hcp (or equivalent).

I quickly passed while alerting the opposition to what partner's bid meant – not that they didn't know – and shamefacedly awaited dummy. The following diagram is what I saw when West led the ♠Q.

Despite my soporific approach, I noticed that the contract had some chances. All I needed was to have the trumps break 3-2 and play for no loser plus the diamonds to come in.

Dealer East– North-South Vulnerable

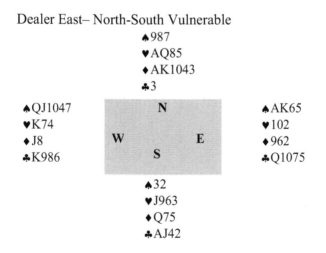

```
                    ♠987
                    ♥AQ85
                    ♦AK1043
                    ♣3
    ♠QJ1047            N            ♠AK65
    ♥K74                             ♥102
    ♦J8          W         E         ♦962
    ♣K986             S             ♣Q1075
                    ♠32
                    ♥J963
                    ♦Q75
                    ♣AJ42
```

I ruffed the third spade and successfully finessed the ♥Q. Since West (an international player) had not claimed one off, I surmised that the ♥10 was not in his hand, so returned to hand with ♣A and placed the ♥J on the table pinning the ♥10.

After drawing trumps, I correctly played the diamonds (unnecessary in this case) and claimed +650. Our poor opponents thought that they had only lost one imp, but not all North-South pairs had bid game, so the loss was even greater.

The opponents had "Ben Blunder" arrive at the table, have a sleep and bid badly and take away the goodies.

Not an advertisement for fairness or balance at the bridge table.

On the following deal, partner (North) bid very conservatively.

WEST	NORTH	EAST	SOUTH
		Pass	1♠
Pass	2♥	Pass	3♦
Pass	4♠	All Pass	

As my 3♦ showed extra strength, I think he should have bid 3♠ after which we could cue bid our way to the good slam. North led the ♣J and I thought at the time that our opposition would bid this slam and that would be the match lost. I was able to make eleven tricks after winning the ♣A and recovering from North showing out on the ♠K at trick two.

Dealer East – All Vulnerable

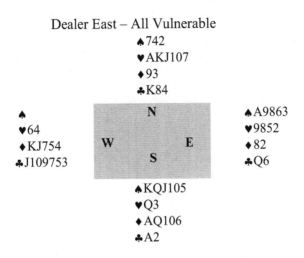

♠742
♥AKJ107
♦93
♣K84

♠
♥64
♦KJ754
♣J109753

♠A9863
♥9852
♦82
♣Q6

♠KQJ105
♥Q3
♦AQ106
♣A2

Well, I was right in respect of the bidding (but wrong thereafter).

Our opposition did outbid us reaching the great slam but they were doubled and one down. I discovered later via Deep Finesse that 6NT by South can make by squeezing West in the minors. Perhaps our team mates shouldn't have doubled?

So they outbid us, but we won and went to the next round and they went home. That doesn't sound a just outcome for them does it? On another day there is a similar occurrence.

Dealer East – All Vulnerable

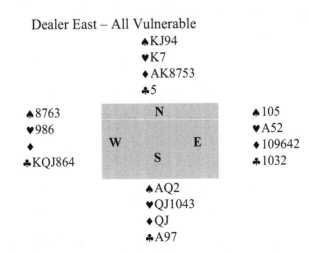

♠KJ94
♥K7
♦AK8753
♣5

♠8763
♥986
♦
♣KQJ864

♠105
♥A52
♦109642
♣1032

♠AQ2
♥QJ1043
♦QJ
♣A97

WEST	NORTH	EAST	SOUTH
		Pass	1NT (1)
Pass	2NT (2)	Pass	3♦ (3)
Pass	3♠	Pass	3NT
All Pass			

1. 15-17 hcp
2. Transfer to diamonds
3. Spade suit and game forcing

West leads the K♣. Partner (South) must be feeling ill as a 6♦ contract looks almost certain. In practice I don't think he noticed, but stoically went about attempting to make nine or more tricks in notrumps.

He ducks two rounds of clubs and starts on diamonds but twitches when West shows out on the first round. He takes his nine tricks and we move on to the next board.

In the score up we get a good score since the field has a lot of good bidders who reached 6♦.

I think his hand has improved with the bidding and he should try a bid of 4♦ over the 3♠ bid enabling us to reach the excellent but failing slam.

Some days luck runs your way.

So, having established that you are only sometimes in control of your bridge destiny, let's look at where we could have done the right thing but usually didn't.

There is ebb and flow during a bridge hand in which there are many chances for all parties to shine, but a lot of the time they become opportunities lost. There are also some hands where the decision to play or defend is not clear until the dust settles.

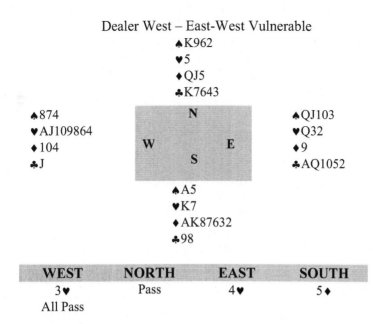

Dealer West – East-West Vulnerable

```
                    ♠K962
                    ♥5
                    ♦QJ5
                    ♣K7643
♠874                  N                ♠QJ103
♥AJ109864                              ♥Q32
♦104         W              E          ♦9
♣J                    S                ♣AQ1052
                    ♠A5
                    ♥K7
                    ♦AK87632
                    ♣98
```

WEST	NORTH	EAST	SOUTH
3♥	Pass	4♥	5♦
All Pass			

West (part of a quality pair) opened 3♥ and East raised to 4♥ (presumably to make at this vulnerability). My partner South did the right thing and bid 5♦ which strangely nobody doubled.

West led the ♣J and East missed a chance to overtake, cash a second club and then the ♥A for a quick one-off (first opportunity).

At this point, West needs to switch to a spade – which is far from obvious – but instead led a diamond (second opportunity).

South won in dummy and led to the ♥K but as expected, the ace was in the West hand. West exited a diamond and South won in hand to ruff his last heart providing the tenth trick.

At this stage, South overlooked a squeeze possibility (it was late in the day and we are Seniors) and conceded one off (third opportunity).

After the play went as it did, South can run all of the diamonds leaving himself with a low spade and the ♣9 opposite the K9 of spades in dummy. With East holding the boss clubs and QJ10 of spades, eleven tricks would have materialised.

Oh well, just another flat board, although we felt better by squandering just one opportunity against their two.

This next deal was a monumental disaster for East-West and a shockingly lucky result for North-South (me as South) which shows that you are better being lucky than good.

WEST	NORTH	EAST	SOUTH
Pass	Pass	1♣	1♥
1♠	4♥	Double	All Pass

The bidding started normally with two passes and 1♣ from East followed by a gentle 1♥ overcall by me as South. West bid 1♠ hoping for a fit either in spades or clubs but implying more points than he had.

Partner (North) then tanked for some time before emerging with a bid of 4♥ which East immediately doubled, expecting to make a small fortune. This became the final contract.

When West led the ♣6, I as South wondered about partner and mentally agreed with East's assessment.

Hoping to cut the losses I ruffed the club and led the ♦2. At this point East erred in a way that will probably haunt him for some time by ducking. The ♦J won and another club was ruffed followed by a spade to the ace (picking up the ♠K) and a final club ruff.

Dealer West – All Vulnerable

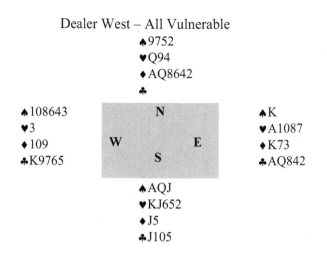

♠9752
♥Q94
♦AQ8642
♣

♠108643   **N**   ♠K
♥3   ♥A1087
♦109   **W**   **E**   ♦K73
♣K9765   **S**   ♣AQ842

♠AQJ
♥KJ652
♦J5
♣J105

The ♦A was led and when East did not drop the king, I thought the best way back to my hand was via spades which East ruffed. The ♦K was now led and I ruffed with the ♥5 which was too high for West confirming that East did indeed hold good pips. Trumps were now led from the top and East ended up with only three tricks, all in Hearts, for -790.

In the ensuing recriminations, East added insult to injury by observing that 5♣ was a make for East-West. Of course, none of the six other pairs involved reached 5♣. I think hands like this are why we play (or not)?

The following deal provided opportunities during the bidding, play and defence.

At my table, the bidding was simple.

WEST	NORTH	EAST	SOUTH
Pass	Pass	Pass	1NT
All Pass			

After three passes I as South and playing a 15-17 1NT range passed up the opportunity to fashionably (or sensibly?) upgrade the hand based on the maximum points and the good 5-card diamond suit. Thus the bidding rested at 1NT and with a club lead, ten tricks resulted. A sequence such as 1♦-1♠; 2NT-3NT would have been very acceptable.

Dealer West – North-South Vulnerable

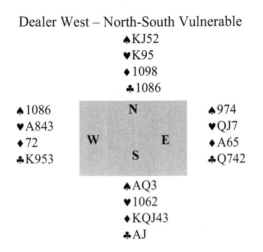

```
              ♠KJ52
              ♥K95
              ♦1098
              ♣1086
♠1086          N          ♠974
♥A843                     ♥QJ7
♦72       W      E        ♦A65
♣K953          S          ♣Q742
              ♠AQ3
              ♥1062
              ♦KQJ43
              ♣AJ
```

At the other table:

WEST	NORTH	EAST	SOUTH
Pass	Pass	Pass	1NT
Pass	2♣	Pass	3♦
Pass	3NT	All Pass	

Their NT range was 15-18 so after South bid 1NT, North was able to inquire about majors and range with South bidding 3♦ (maximum and 5-card diamond suit) allowing North to bid 3NT. At this stage there was no opportunity lost.

West had been listening to the bidding and led the ♥3. Declarer who really didn't want a club switch and who knew that the lead was fourth best, could/should have risen with the ♥K, her opportunity to guarantee the contract. But she didn't.

East now had the opportunity for the club switch to ensure victory for the defence. However, declarer (presumably by design) had played the ♥6 at trick one, hiding the ♥2 and creating the possibility that West had a 5-card suit. On this basis, East continued hearts and the game was made.

Another example of the subtleties and ebb and flow of a bridge deal.

This was an odd deal.

Dealer North – East-West Vulnerable

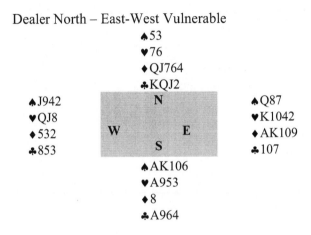

```
                    ♠53
                    ♥76
                    ♦QJ764
                    ♣KQJ2
    ♠J942               N              ♠Q87
    ♥QJ8                               ♥K1042
    ♦532          W         E          ♦AK109
    ♣853               S              ♣107
                    ♠AK106
                    ♥A953
                    ♦8
                    ♣A964
```

The bidding:

WEST	NORTH	EAST	SOUTH
	Pass	Pass	1♣
Pass	1♦	1♥	1♠
Pass	3♣	Pass	5♣
All Pass			

First of all East passed. I think she was distracted by something else in the room because I know she normally loves to bid as often as possible.

I (as South) opened 1♣ and North bid his suit with 1♦. East had since re-looked at her hand and bid 1♥ and I bid 1♠ – consistent with a 4-4-1-4 or 4-3-1-5 type hand. Partner took a rosy view (easier on the assumption that I had five clubs) with his 3♣ and I (after some thought) assumed partner had a 5-5 in the minors and 10-11 hcp and so bid the game.

As you can see, this was not a good series of decisions. West quickly led the ♥Q (first opportunity to lead a trump) and I took the Ace and led my diamond. East could have led a trump (second opportunity) but cashed the ♥K and instead of now leading a trump (third opportunity) led a third heart. I was now able to crossruff the rest (since the ♣10 was in the East hand) and claimed the contract and plus 400.

This turned out to be an important result as, at the other table:

WEST	NORTH	EAST	SOUTH
	Pass	1♦	Double
All Pass			

Our East opened 1♦, South doubled and North left it in. The defence slipped at that table achieving only one off (- 200 instead of -500). Another opportunity lost.

Perhaps the East at our table wasn't distracted after all but had foreseen the danger of opening this hand?

This deal was an example of muddled thinking by me but not the opposition.

Dealer East – North-South Vulnerable

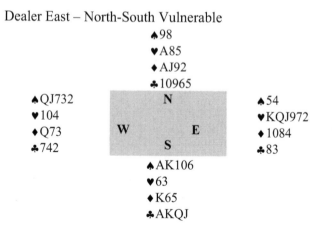

                   ♠98
                   ♥A85
                   ♦AJ92
                   ♣10965

♠QJ732   N   ♠54
♥104   ♥KQJ972
♦Q73   W   E   ♦1084
♣742   S   ♣83

                   ♠AK106
                   ♥63
                   ♦K65
                   ♣AKQJ

At my table, East opened 2♦ showing 3-7 hcp and a 6-card major and I as South doubled. West bid 3♥, pass or correct, partner doubled and East passed. What is best?

WEST	NORTH	EAST	SOUTH
		2♦	Double
3♥	Double	Pass	4♠
All Pass			

I assumed wrongly that partner was making a take-out of Hearts. This is not logical since West had shown a high tolerance for Spades with the 3♥ bid. A bid of 3NT was possible but I catastrophically bid 4♠.

The opponent in our match faced the same situation but the bidding continued as follows:

WEST	NORTH	EAST	SOUTH
		2♦	Double
3♥	Double	Pass	4♥
Pass	4NT	Pass	6♣
All Pass			

In my position South bid 4♥ and North bid 4NT and they settled in 6♣ for a good outcome.

Six out of eight ended in 3NT while the results in our match – minus 200 in 4♠ and plus 1390 in 6♣ were unique. In a funny way, my blunder didn't cost as much as it might have compared to my bidding 3NT.

On reflection, their bids were far superior and they deserved the pick-up.

At the time, I was a bit surprised by the 3♥ bid by West, but she knew we were close to a slam and was being pre-emptive – good thinking.

On this deal, the opposition struck gold with their early pre-empt.

Dealer East – Nil Vulnerability

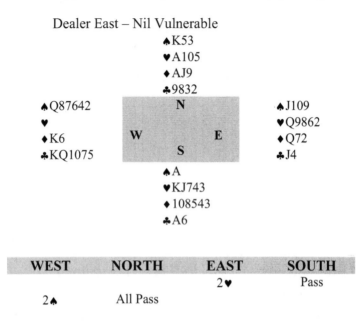

                        ♠K53
                        ♥A105
                        ♦AJ9
                        ♣9832
♠Q87642   N   ♠J109
♥   ♥Q9862
♦K6   W   E   ♦Q72
♣KQ1075   S   ♣J4
                        ♠A
                        ♥KJ743
                        ♦108543
                        ♣A6

WEST	NORTH	EAST	SOUTH
		2♥	Pass
2♠	All Pass		

East opened 2♥ showing 6-10 hcp and a 5 or 6-card major. South passed and West bid 2♠ passed around to South who also passed.

As unattractive as it looks, South has to bid at this stage and to me 3♦ looks the only choice. I don't like double as an option although that doesn't make it wrong. I as North would bid 3NT and equity would be restored.

West made nine tricks and we were the only pair who weren't in game or doubling 4♠.

Tough game and another lost opportunity.

This next deal prompted much discussion with probably both bidders at fault (partner and me), but a hand worth considering for style.

Dealer North – North South Vulnerable

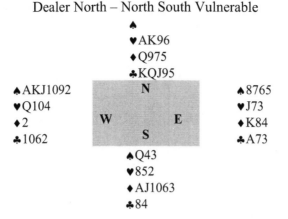

```
              ♠
              ♥AK96
              ♦Q975
              ♣KQJ95
♠AKJ1092         N           ♠8765
♥Q104                        ♥J73
♦2          W        E       ♦K84
♣1062            S           ♣A73
              ♠Q43
              ♥852
              ♦AJ1063
              ♣84
```

The bidding:

WEST	NORTH	EAST	SOUTH
	1♣	Pass	1♦ (1)
1♠	2♥ (2)	2♠	Pass
Pass	3♦ (3)	All Pass	

1. At the time this deal came up, my partner and I had played together a lot, but not in recent times. In any case, my understanding is that we don't bid 1♦ ahead of a major unless we have a strong follow up or are single-suited.
2. Partner's reverse should be at least 5 clubs and 4 hearts and say 17+ hcp. This hand certainly qualifies.
3. Partner bids out his shape, although it is possible that he is 1-4-3-5 shape.

We play in a part score while twelve tricks are easily made – missing 620 or 1370 in favour of 170. Strangely enough we have a pick-up in a Teams event with our partners losing -100 in 4♠ untroubled.
There is a case for me as South to move to at least 4♦ over 3♦ since I know partner to be a conservative. However as the author in charge of this text, I consider that North's second bids of 4♦, 5♦ or 3♠ (splinter) all rank much more highly than the one chosen.

Whatever you think and despite the pick-up on the score sheet, this was another Opportunity Lost.

This deal is worth talking about.

Dealer South – All Vulnerable

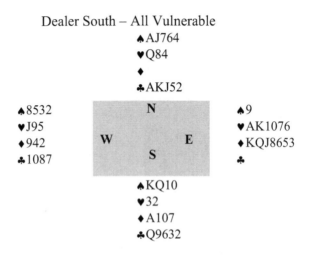

```
                    ♠AJ764
                    ♥Q84
                    ♦
                    ♣AKJ52
    ♠8532            N            ♠9
    ♥J95                          ♥AK1076
    ♦942      W          E        ♦KQJ8653
    ♣1087           S             ♣
                    ♠KQ10
                    ♥32
                    ♦A107
                    ♣Q9632
```

The bidding was the product of a complex system where doubt arises early on.

If I recall, South opened 1♠ showing 8-12hcp and no 4-card major. North bid 2♥ transfer to spades and my partner (East) doubled to show hearts. A bid of 2♠ (Michaels) here would have been more descriptive. South showed his 3-card spade support with a 2♠ bid with North passing and partner now bidding 3♦. North competed to 3♠ and East bid 4♦. South passed and North bid 4♠ with partner competing to 5♦. South now bid 5♠ and that ended the bidding.

WEST	NORTH	EAST	SOUTH
			1♠
Pass	2♥	Double	2♠
Pass	Pass	3♦	Pass
Pass	3♠	4♦	Pass
Pass	4♠	5♦	5♠
All Pass			

Partner had shown extreme shape, but failed to double (which could have been Lightner for an unusual lead) and I woodenly led a diamond. Declarer thankfully took his eleven tricks and partner admonished me for not leading a club, which led to a Lightner discussion. There is no doubt that a diamond was wrong, but if partner doesn't double, then isn't he denying a trump?

Much later with the help of all hands on view, I realised that I missed yet another opportunity for both partner and me to shine. The ♥J lead can do the trick. If declarer covers, then partner can win trick one and underlead to my ♥9. This unusual play would now prompt a club switch for a one trick defeat and a brilliancy award.

Of course, if partner took me for doubleton jack in hearts and tried to give me a third round ruff, then declarer would be the winner yet again. Overall, I think if you want a ruff, you should double. Note that their bidding system gave me the chance for fame by making South declarer which wasn't usually the case.

In any case, my dumb diamond lead killed the many opportunities available, so who cares what I think? By the bye, the range of contracts across a largish field spanned from doubled making part scores, doubled unsuccessful games through to successful contracts up the six diamonds level (a contract that shows extreme optimism).

The next exhibit was a deal where all others contributed while I was a bystander. After two passes, South opened 1♣. As West I overcalled 1♥ with the following:

♠K64
♥KQ986
♦J105
♣97

So far so good. North bid 1NT, partner passed and South reversed with
2♦. North persisted with 2NT and South reluctantly raised to 3NT.

WEST	NORTH	EAST	SOUTH
	Pass	Pass	1♣
1♥	1NT	Pass	2♦
Pass	2NT	Pass	3NT
All Pass			

The full hand:

Dealer North – Nil Vulnerable

```
                    ♠A103
                    ♥J743
                    ♦732
                    ♣AJ5
        ♠K64          N          ♠875
        ♥KQ986                   ♥A1052
        ♦J105     W     E        ♦984
        ♣97          S           ♣1043
                    ♠QJ92
                    ♥
                    ♦AKQ6
                    ♣KQ862
```

Well, this looks simple doesn't it? Partner leads the ♥2 and the contract
goes one-off – a just result for the putrid opposition bidding (from a
pair with international credentials – not in use here).

Well that's not what happened. Partner had a brain wave and led a
diamond. North smugly and safely claims ten tricks. I have to point out
to partner and declarer that the ♥2 is a more successful lead– neither of
them recognised that at the time.

Meanwhile, South observes that 7♣ is gin and that 6♣ would be more
than sensible. I am not happy but hope that my team mates reach the
slam zone.

Not to be – they stop at 5♣ and make thirteen.

I wasn't a happy bystander but nevertheless retain though not without a struggle – a philosophical approach to lost opportunities at the bridge table.

The next deal occurred during the 1995 National Open Teams in Canberra Australia and the story arose because my then wife and I had equally good tales to tell. After South opened 1♥, West bid 2NT for the minors and South ended in 5♥.

Dealer South, North-South Vulnerable

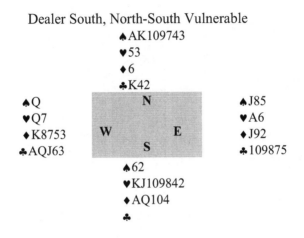

When I was declarer, West led the ♠Q which is the **only** correct card to beat the contract (check it out on Deep Finesse).
Since I couldn't see any technical line to make the contract I thought I would seek help from the defenders by leading a trump after capturing the ♠Q (appearing to clear trumps before suffering a spade ruff. Sure enough, East rose to the occasion by winning with the ace.

At this stage North only has to lead a second trump to defeat me but thought he 'foiled' my plan by leading a spade. West did get his ruff but now, unfortunately for the defence, was endplayed. West tried the ♣A (a low club or any diamond is no better) and after ruffing this card, I was able to play ♦A, ruff a diamond and discard my two diamond losers on the ♣K and ♠K.

At my wife's table where she was a defender, her partner led the ♣A which looks bad (and is bad), but it got better. South won the next four tricks with two diamond ruffs and the ♣K and a club ruff, but after this sequence found himself in dummy, as follows:

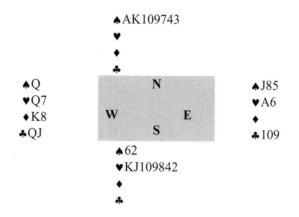

♠AK109743
♥
♦
♣

♠Q
♥Q7
♦K8
♣QJ

N
W   E
S

♠J85
♥A6
♦
♣109

♠62
♥KJ109842
♦
♣

He tried two rounds of spades, but South ruffed with the seven and led a winning diamond.

East ruffed this with the ♥A and played a third spade promoting the ♥Q en passant for the setting trick.

Having since consulted Deep Finesse at length, I now know that declarer could have made the contract in a number of ways after the ♣A lead, but didn't – otherwise the story would not be as good.

This next deal was neat where both declarer and defender shone at opposite tables. Even though my team lost at both tables, it was instructive to watch.

Dealer West, North-South Vulnerable

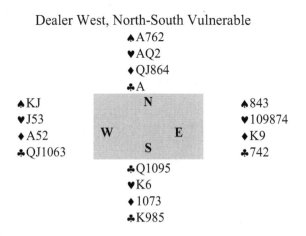

```
                    ♠A762
                    ♥AQ2
                    ♦QJ864
                    ♣A
  ♠KJ             N              ♠843
  ♥J53                           ♥109874
  ♦A52       W         E         ♦K9
  ♣QJ1063         S              ♣742
                    ♣Q1095
                    ♥K6
                    ♦1073
                    ♣K985
```

At our table, West bid 1♣ and North doubled with South eventually ending in 4♠. West made the safe lead of ♣Q – or so he thought.

Declarer made short work by playing three rounds of hearts pitching a diamond (!) to prevent a third round ruff. The ace and another spade put West on lead with no good options. A low diamond at trick one is the simplest defence, but strangely enough a low club at trick one works equally well (oh yeah!) since South holds the K985. If West leads a club honour, he becomes endplayed later in clubs after three rounds of hearts pitching the diamond and two spades. Exiting a diamond at that stage does no harm Minus 620.

At the other table the contract and lead was the same, but declarer attacked trumps first and a clever West (Martin Bloom) on winning the ♠K did indeed find the low diamond switch for the contract defeat.

West did very well, but my prize goes to the declarer who saw the risk and took an early diamond pitch.

The next deal had a few pleasant surprises.

Dealer West, East-West Vulnerable

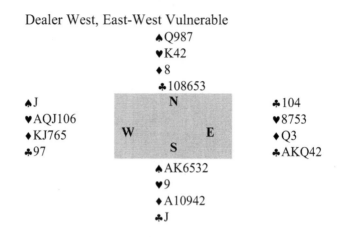

♠Q987
♥K42
♦8
♣108653

♠J
♥AQJ106
♦KJ765
♣97

♣104
♥8753
♦Q3
♣AKQ42

♠AK6532
♥9
♦A10942
♣J

West opened 1♥ and I passed as North. East bid 2NT (Jacoby – 4 plus hearts and game-force) and partner surprised me with a 4♠ bid.

I thought he would be weaker for this action and in subsequent conversations suggested other bids such as double (not preferred) and 3♥ (Michaels). Mind you, his bid also features in the conversation. Anyway, after West bid 5♥ I bid 5♠ valuing my hand as being quite strong for the weakest hand at the table.

WEST	NORTH	EAST	SOUTH
1♥	Pass	2NT	4♠
5♥	5♠	Double	All Pass

As you can see, 5♥ X can go for 500 which is better than our making game – but we are now in 5♠ X.

West led the ♥A and then switched to the ♣9 taken by the ♣Q followed by a low diamond taken by the ace.

Fortunately for us, the club nine and seven were doubleton and declarer was able to set up dummy's clubs with ruffing finesses thus making plus 590. So this was one of those happy surprises despite the early adverse outlook.

A case of an opportunity retrieved from a doubtful situation.

The declarer at our table won the bidding on the next deal but erred in the play at trick two. The required defence is spectacular.

East (me) opened the bidding with 1♥ and South ended proceedings with a leap to 4♠.

WEST	NORTH	EAST	SOUTH
		1♥	4♠

All Pass

Partner obediently led the ♥9 and North won the ace. As you can see an immediate finesse of the ♠J leads to success, however this declarer decided to play East for ♠Ax and played to the king. Alas for him, West took the ace and led another heart.

North after ruffing my ♥Q re-thought his strategy, first weighing up options of dropping the ♠J or the ♣Q, but then coming up with an alternative of leading a low club to establish the ♣J as an entry for a second spade finesse. This is not without risk but is worth a shot and works on this layout.

Dealer East, Nil Vulnerable

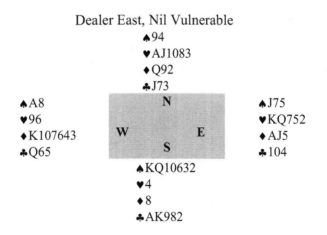

```
                    ♠94
                    ♥AJ1083
                    ♦Q92
                    ♣J73
    ♠A8              N              ♠J75
    ♥96                             ♥KQ752
    ♦K107643    W        E         ♦AJ5
    ♣Q65             S              ♣104
                    ♠KQ10632
                    ♥4
                    ♦8
                    ♣AK982
```

Partner rose with the ♣Q and after some thought decided to play the ♦K. It is here that the narrative gets weird. I eschewed letting partner take this trick, but instead overtook with the ace♦ (setting up dummy's ♦Q) and played the ♥K which promoted a trump trick for me as the setting trick (I cover the ♠9 setting up the ♠7 if declarer enter dummy to lead the spade).

Of course, as befits this chapter heading, this is all a fantasy – declarer quietly going down by failing to drop either the ♠J or ♣Q and rueing not taking the immediate ♠J finesse.

Meanwhile, Deep Finesse and I are enjoying each other's company while I am constantly daydreaming of ways to win the Defence of the Year Award.

Okay enough of what might have been, let's get straight to the slam zone which is one of the more exciting areas of bidding and play for Joe Average.

3   Chapter 3 – Slamming Along

We all like to bid slams. There is an added excitement when we do, something akin to watching a trapeze act at the circus. Here are some that were bid and others that weren't.

North opens a Precision club (17+hcp any shape) and East overcalls 3♣ (disruptive). After South bids 3♥ (game force) various cues follow and South pushes on to 6♥ despite the further bidding identifying that the opposition have the ♦A.

WEST	NORTH	EAST	SOUTH
	1♣	3♣	3♥
Pass	cue	Pass	cue
Pass	cue	Pass	6♥
All Pass			

Dealer North – Nil Vulnerable

```
                  ♠6
                  ♥AK95
                  ♦KQJ94
                  ♣AQ9
  ♠QJ93              N           ♠8542
  ♥832                           ♥10
  ♦A10865    W           E       ♦73
  ♣6                 S           ♣KJ10743
                  ♠AK107
                  ♥QJ764
                  ♦2
                  ♣852
```

After a Heart lead won in dummy by the ace with East showing the singleton ten, North establishes diamonds for club discards and despite a second trump lead is able to crossruff the rest. The play goes the same way on the singleton club lead at any stage.

If a club is led originally, North wins the ace, plays one round of trumps and establishes diamonds with West unable to lead a second club. Even if West ducks the first diamond, South persists for two club discards.

This means that North really should be playing it if East has the ♦A. The following deal showed my unadventurous side. Some say boring!

Dealer East – All Vulnerable

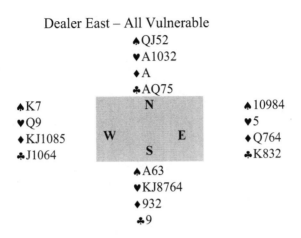

      ♠QJ52
      ♥A1032
      ♦A
      ♣AQ75

♠K7   **N**   ♠10984
♥Q9   ♥5
♦KJ1085 **W** **E** ♦Q764
♣J1064   **S**   ♣K832

      ♠A63
      ♥KJ8764
      ♦932
      ♣9

East passed and South (partner) bid 2♥ (showing 8-11hcp and 6-card suit). I raised to 4♥ which proved too little. No one in a small field bid this one.

On reflection I should have inquired with 2NT (strong inquiry), received a 3♣ bid showing club shortage. I could then cue 3♦ and South can follow with a 3♠ cue after which 6♥ is a reasonable final bid.

This next deal was interesting. No-one bid to the best spot of seven hearts. In fact only one table out of fourteen played it in hearts.

You don't want to be in 7♠ missing the ♠Q, but the heart grand is fairly easy with two spade pitches in the South hand and a club ruff in the North hand.

Dealer East– North-South Vulnerable

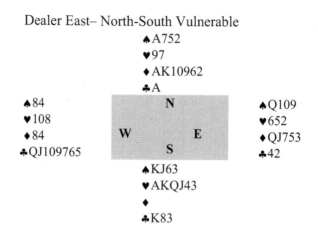

```
                    ♠A752
                    ♥97
                    ♦AK10962
                    ♣A
    ♠84              N              ♠Q109
    ♥108                            ♥652
    ♦84        W         E          ♦QJ753
    ♣QJ109765          S            ♣42
                    ♠KJ63
                    ♥AKQJ43
                    ♦
                    ♣K83
```

A suggested sequence using a simple system:

WEST	NORTH	EAST	SOUTH
		Pass	1♥
Pass	2♦	Pass	2♠ (1)
Pass	3♠ (2)	Pass	4NT (3)
Pass	5♦ (4)	Pass	5♥ (5)
Pass	5♠(6)	Pass	5NT (7)
Pass	6♦ (8)	Pass	7♥ (9)
All Pass			

1. Usually showing extra strength
2. Strong support showing slam interest.
3. RKCB
4. 0 or 3 Keycards (obviously 3)
5. Do you have the Q♠?
6. No
7. Any Kings?
8. ♦K
9. We have arrived – no conversion please.

The next deal was an interesting one bid by the opposition with my thoughts attached.

South opened with an artificial two level bid showing either majors or minors and they settled in 4♠ making twelve after North bid 3 ♦ pass or correct. North opined that the South hand was a one bid. This looks the best option. Four out of six pairs in the field were in slam.

Dealer East – East-West Vulnerable

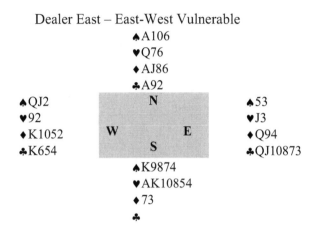

```
                    ♠A106
                    ♥Q76
                    ♦AJ86
                    ♣A92
    ♠QJ2            N            ♠53
    ♥92                          ♥J3
    ♦K1052    W         E        ♦Q94
    ♣K654          S             ♣QJ10873
                    ♠K9874
                    ♥AK10854
                    ♦73
                    ♣
```

If South opens 1♥ and after a 2♦ reply could bid 2♠ without showing extra values then the slam should be reached. Of course, South could value the hand as a strong one and re-bid 2♠ showing extra values in which case slam would be mandatory.

However, if South rebids 2♥ to show a more limited type opening, then game would probably be the limit.

On reflection even after the two opening, North should have bid 2NT to seek more information (usually an invitational strength bid).

The North hand is comfortable with either the major or minor option. Then South could easily bid 3♠ to show the top of the range and a 6-5 type of hand. A 5NT pick a slam bid by North would allow 6♥ to be easily reached which seems to have more chances although both spade and heart contracts make on this occasion.

Thus, depending on system agreements there is more than one way to bid this one.

This next deal needed successful play to bring home the bacon.

Dealer West – East-West Vulnerable

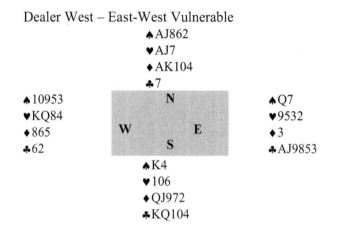

```
                    ♠ AJ862
                    ♥ AJ7
                    ♦ AK104
                    ♣ 7
  ♠ 10953              N              ♠ Q7
  ♥ KQ84                              ♥ 9532
  ♦ 865        W           E         ♦ 3
  ♣ 62                  S             ♣ AJ9853
                    ♠ K4
                    ♥ 106
                    ♦ QJ972
                    ♣ KQ104
```

West passed and North opened a strong club (17+) with us eventually settling for six diamonds by South.

Partner (Chris Sundstrom) played well winning the ♥K lead, and playing ♠K and ♠A setting up the ♠J immediately. Two rounds of trumps ended in dummy for the heart pitch (leaving a trump outstanding).

A small club was now led and East took his ace, ending proceedings. If he ducks, then North can cross-ruff setting up the fifth spade and use it to pitch his last club with East winning the only trick for the defence with the thirteenth trump. Very cute. Five bid it but only two succeeded. Good on you pard.

Partner later tells me that he once read a book – shades of Mollo's Rueful Rabbit – about establishing the side suit before drawing trumps to explain why he tried to ruff out the spades instead of taking the finesse. In this case – quite unlike Rueful Rabbit – a relevant book play at the right time.

This was one fish that got away.

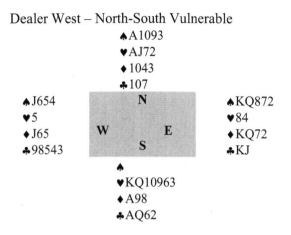

♠A1093
♥AJ72
♦1043
♣107

♠J654
♥5
♦J65
♣98543

♠KQ872
♥84
♦KQ72
♣KJ

♠
♥KQ10963
♦A98
♣AQ62

After two passes, East bid 1♠ and I as South overcalled 2♥. West passed and North raised to 4♥ stating that he was light for the bid (after the bidding concluded of course). Six was easy with the club finesse and I didn't even investigate. One other pair out of six did bid it.

Probably I should have doubled first which would better show that I did indeed have a strong hand. Alternatively and more simply, I should assume that partner has either four trumps or a good hand for his 4♥ bid. In this case, he could easily hold the heart ace and the king in either one of the minor suits, so the slam should a good chance and I should have investigated further.

Another case of lower level unimaginative thinking.
While I am in a confessional mode here is another mistake of mine compounded by my partner's misunderstanding of my bidding. This was our first game together so there is always the certainty of some misunderstandings. I held:

♠AQ965432
♥AK6
♦
♣KQ

Quite a good hand you would agree? I was besotted with my eight card spade suit and allowed my judgement to be clouded. Also, I couldn't imagine placing my hand down as dummy, and there's the rub.

The bidding went as follows (from my point of view):

Dealer South, East-West Vulnerable

WEST	NORTH	EAST	SOUTH
			2♣ (1)
Pass	2♥ (2)	Pass	3♠ (3)
Pass	4♦ (4)	Pass	4NT (5)
Pass	5♥ (6)	Pass	6♠ (7)
All Pass			

1. Artificial Game Force
2. A positive showing 1.5 Honour Tricks (i.e. an ace and a king or three kings plus four or more hearts).
3. Setting Spades as the trump suit
4. Cue bid agreeing spades
5. RKCB
6. Two Keycards in spades (i.e. the spade king and the diamond ace)
7. Content and confident

The full hand

Dealer South – East-West Vulnerable

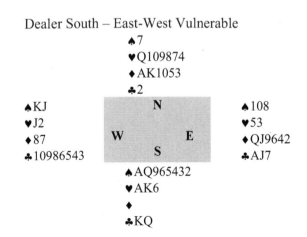

```
                  ♠7
                  ♥Q109874
                  ♦AK1053
                  ♣2
    ♠KJ              N          ♠108
    ♥J2                         ♥53
    ♦87         W       E       ♦QJ9642
    ♣10986543         S         ♣AJ7
                  ♠AQ965432
                  ♥AK6
                  ♦
                  ♣KQ
```

Here I was one down whereas 5♠ makes and more importantly so does 6♥! There were a lot of better bidders than me in the room reaching the right slam. So I should have been destined to be dummy.

So some explanation is required. My new partner agreed on bids 1 and 2, but here's what he thought about the rest.

3. He has a good suit in spades
4. My second suit
5. RKC in diamonds as the last bid suit
6. Two Keycards in diamonds
7. I am sure he knows what he is doing.

With a little more thought and humility, here is a sequence that could have happened.

WEST	NORTH	EAST	SOUTH
			2♣ (1)
Pass	2♥ (2)	Pass	2♠ (3)
Pass	3♦ (4)	Pass	3♥ (5)
Pass	4♥ (6)	Pass	4NT (7)
Pass	5♣ (8)	Pass	5♦ (9)
Pass	6♦ (10)	Pass	6♥ (11)
All Pass			

1. Artificial Game Force
2. A positive showing 1.5 Honour Tricks (i.e. an ace and a king or three kings plus four or more hearts).
3. Spades
4. Second suit
5. Setting hearts
6. Despite my extra shape, I have no more to say at present
7. RKCB in hearts
8. 1 or 4 Keycards
9. Do you have the ♥Q?
10. Yes and the diamond ace
11. We have arrived!

This sequence identifies a losing club regardless of who holds the ♠K although the 6♦ bid may have denied that card.

At the same tournament there were several other eight card suits suggesting some spice in the dealing machine.

Example 1

```
        ♠
        ♥1062
        ♦97
        ♣AKQ98762
```

This is the bidding preceding your decision.

Dealer East – All Vulnerable

WEST	NORTH	EAST	SOUTH
		1♠	1NT
4♠	Your bid?		

Partner bid 5♣ which ended the auction but soon regretted the decision as evidenced by the full hand. He may have been influenced by my lack of success with an eight card suit earlier?

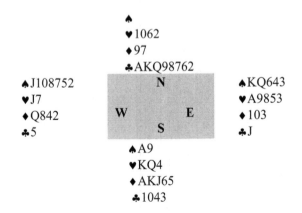

```
              ♠
              ♥1062
              ♦97
              ♣AKQ98762
♠J108752          N          ♠KQ643
♥J7                           ♥A9853
♦Q842      W         E        ♦103
♣5                  S         ♣J
              ♠A9
              ♥KQ4
              ♦AKJ65
              ♣1043
```

Example 2 – Later in the tournament I picked up the following hand:

♠53
♥6
♦QJ
♣AKJ109754

Dealer West – East-West Vulnerable

WEST	NORTH	EAST	SOUTH
Pass	1♦	Pass	2♣
Pass	2♠	Pass	My bid?

My partner's reverse showed a strong hand and my diamonds improved in quality with the bidding, so without further ado I bid 6♣. Twelve tricks proved easy this time with 13 available with the right finesse.

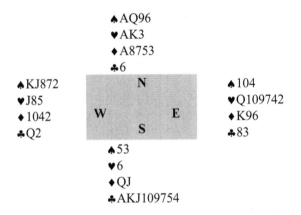

Same tournament, one more slam that should have been easy, but being a Senior I think my partner was having a little sleep at the table.

Partner bid a game force 2♣ and my 2♦ was a negative. He elected to bid 2NT which was very fortuitous since I could now transfer to spades showing at least 5 cards in the suit. This should have had him leaping from his seat with visions of slam. All I needed was the ♠K or the A and the ♠J.

WEST	NORTH	EAST	SOUTH
Pass	2♣	Pass	2♦
Pass	2NT	Pass	3♥
Pass	3♠	Pass	3NT
Pass	4♠	All Pass	

Dealer West – All Vulnerable

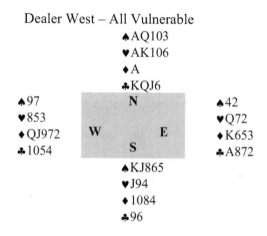

```
                    ♠AQ103
                    ♥AK106
                    ♦A
                    ♣KQJ6
   ♠97              N              ♠42
   ♥853                            ♥Q72
   ♦QJ972      W         E         ♦K653
   ♣1054              S            ♣A872
                    ♠KJ865
                    ♥J94
                    ♦1084
                    ♣96
```

He should not have merely bid 3♠ which on a very bad day I could pass. Nor should he have settled for 4♠ only.

This was a case for bad seating arrangements. If I had held his hand I would have asked for Keycards immediately after the transfer and easily reached the slam.

Strangely enough only 6 out of 36 tables bid this slam. Very puzzling.

On this next deal, the opposition against us spent a long time thinking about bidding slam, but stopped in 5♣. I was very pleased about their decision. Disappointingly our team mates didn't bid it either. I think it is easy.

Dealer South, East-West Vulnerable

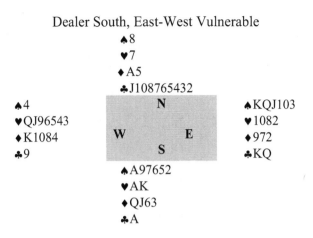

```
                  ♠8
                  ♥7
                  ◆A5
                  ♣J108765432
        ♠4          N          ♠KQJ103
        ♥QJ96543              ♥1082
        ◆K1084    W     E      ◆972
        ♣9          S          ♣KQ
                  ♠A97652
                  ♥AK
                  ◆QJ63
                  ♣A
```

South opened 1♠ and West bid 3♥. North with his 9-bagger and a spare ace should bid 5♣ and South should bid six without too much thought. This sequence did occur at another table.

With this next deal I reveal a smug outcome for me.

We are playing against opponents I am always happy to see leave our table. Worse, they are getting the better of us in the match when this hand comes along. I am North and hold the following cards.

Dealer East – North South Vulnerable
```
                  ♠K4
                  ♥1084
                  ◆AJ65
                  ♣A1084
```

East opens with a 4♣ bid and the explanation is purposely very convoluted in an attempt to confuse the situation (only a few players bring out my paranoia), but I interpret the bid to mean a club pre-empt. Partner doubles, South passes and I actually don't know what to do. Eventually I emerge with 4NT and quick as a flash partner bids 5◆. It's my turn again and I still don't know what to do, but optimistically bid 6◆.

WEST	NORTH	EAST	SOUTH
		4♣	Double
Pass	4NT	Pass	5♦
Pass	6♦	All Pass	

The full hand is:

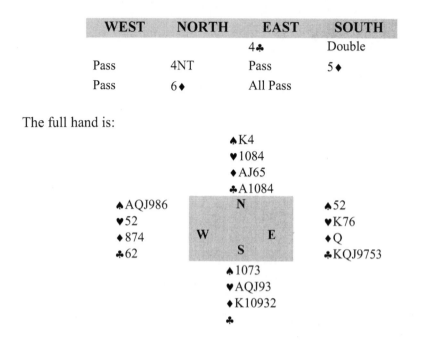

       ♠K4
       ♥1084
       ♦AJ65
       ♣A1084

♠AQJ986   **N**   ♠52
♥52   ♥K76
♦874   **W**   **E**   ♦Q
♣62   **S**   ♣KQJ9753

       ♠1073
       ♥AQJ93
       ♦K10932
       ♣

West leads a club and the play is quick and successful with the ♦Q showing up immediately and the heart finesse working. While it is not necessarily a great slam, chalk one up for the good guys. And I secretly, sweetly and smugly note that we were pushed into it by the pre-empt.

Partner also confides later that he thought he had hesitated too long over the pre-empt, so felt obliged to bid something. I think he must bid and his double is probably better than, say, 4NT (showing just a two-suiter).

Here's a diversion with some idle observations.

On the same night two other low points diamond slams were available on minimum points, but rarely bid (shown here as suitable examples of the genre).

Dealer East – both Vulnerable

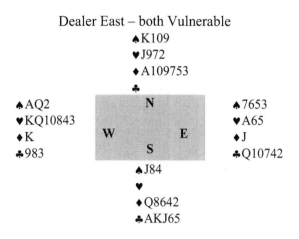

           ♠K109
           ♥J972
           ♦A109753
           ♣

♠AQ2   ♠7653
♥KQ10843   ♥A65
♦K   ♦J
♣983   ♣Q10742

           ♠J84
           ♥
           ♦Q8642
           ♣AKJ65

After East passed, South opened 1♦ and I as West overcalled 1♥.
North then finished the auction with a 5♦ bid. Six was easy with the
spade ace with West and the diamonds falling.

As an aside, this deal was also specifically reported by Matthew
Thomson in his book "How to Be a Lucky Player" in which he extols
the undoubted skills of the late Bobby Richman. Matthew describes
how Bobby as North recognising the great playing strength of the North
hand bid 6♦ after an auction where East-West showed lots of hearts
following South's 1♦ opening.

On this next deal, East opened 4♠ and South bid 4NT. North settled for
5♦ and was untroubled in the play to make six despite the 4-0 trump
break but having the clubs break 3-3.

Dealer East – East-West Vulnerable

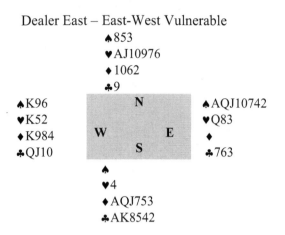

♠853
♥AJ10976
♦1062
♣9

♠K96
♥K52
♦K984
♣QJ10

♠AQJ10742
♥Q83
♦
♣763

♠
♥4
♦AQJ753
♣AK8542

Would you have been bold enough for the top prize for these little gems?

The next three slams were from an Interstate Seniors' Team competition held in Hobart, Australia in 2002.

Dealer North – North-South Vulnerable

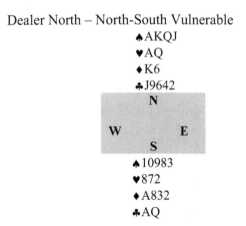

♠AKQJ
♥AQ
♦K6
♣J9642

♠10983
♥872
♦A832
♣AQ

After East passed first in hand the uninterrupted bidding went as follows:

1♣ – 1♠; 4♠ showing 19-20 or four losers. Richard Cowan valued his aces and concentrated club values and moved on to 6♠, making seven with both kings onside, but with plenty of chances otherwise.

Dealer South, North-South Vulnerable

♠Q632
♥5
♦QJ943
♣K95

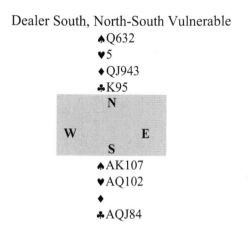

♠AK107
♥AQ102
♦
♣AQJ84

WEST	NORTH	EAST	SOUTH
			2♣
Pass	2♦	Pass	3♣
Pass	4♣	Pass	4NT
Pass	5♦	Pass	6♣
All Pass			

2♣ was game force, 2♦ was 0-1 control, 3♣ was a suit and 4♣ was stronger than 5♣, then Roman Keycard showing one (♣K). The result was +1390 with spades being 3-2 and clubs 4-1 and West having ♥K J 9 tight. This is an example of a 5-3 fit playing better than a 4-4 fit since the ruffs are in the short holding with plenty of entries to the long holding.

Dealer East, Nil Vulnerable

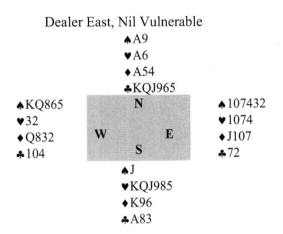

♠A9
♥A6
♦A54
♣KQJ965

♠KQ865
♥32
♦Q832
♣104

♠107432
♥1074
♦J107
♣72

♠J
♥KQJ985
♦K96
♣A83

The bidding:

WEST	NORTH	EAST	SOUTH
		Pass	1♥
Pass	2♣	Pass	2♥
Pass	4NT	Pass	5♠
Pass	7♣	All Pass	

North's 2♣ was natural and game forcing and South's 2♥ indicated six cards in the suit as 2NT and other bids were available. Roman Keycard identified the ♥K and Q and the ♣A, but did not identify the ♥J, hence 7♣. South could easily have bid 7♥ or 7NT, but did not.

As dummy tracked, I as North suggested a potential 2-3 imp loss, but as 6♥ was the limit of bidding in the other room, it was a 9 imp pickup.

This hand demonstrates the power of a double fit.

Dealer South, Both Vulnerable

```
              ♠J2
              ♥K1063
              ♦A108764
              ♣8
  ♠K103              N            ♠9864
  ♥85                             ♥J7
  ♦Q5        W           E        ♦9
  ♣K75432             S           ♣AQJ1096
              ♠AQ75
              ♥AQ942
              ♦KJ32
              ♣
```

The bidding can go many ways depending on system. The following is an example using Bergen raises of a major:

WEST	NORTH	EAST	SOUTH
			1♥
Pass	3♦ (1)	Pass	3♠ (2)
Pass	4♦ (3)	Pass	6♥
All Pass			

1. Artificial bid – Upgraded to 9-11hcp range with 4 hearts
2. Natural
3. Cue

This misses 7♦ on the actual layout. The bulletin from the tournament suggested the following sequence:

WEST	NORTH	EAST	SOUTH
			1♥
Pass	3♦ (1)	Pass	3♠ (2)
Pass	4♦ (3)	Pass	4NT (4)
Pass	5♥ (5)	Pass	7♦ (6)
All Pass			

1. Fit showing jump
2. cue
3. cue
4. RKCB in diamonds knowing there is no wastage in clubs
5. 2 key cards
6. planning to take discards on the hearts.

This hand was very satisfying in the bidding and play, although not in the score up.

Dealer East, Nil Vulnerable

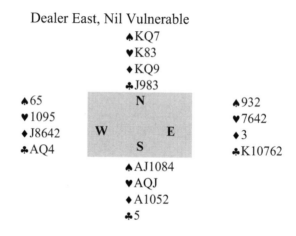

```
              ♠KQ7
              ♥K83
              ♦KQ9
              ♣J983
  ♠65            N            ♠932
  ♥1095                       ♥7642
  ♦J8642     W       E        ♦3
  ♣AQ4            S            ♣K10762
              ♠AJ1084
              ♥AQJ
              ♦A1052
              ♣5
```

The bidding went as follows:

WEST	NORTH	EAST	SOUTH
		Pass	1♠
Pass	2♣ (1)	Pass	2♦
Pass	2♥ (2)	Pass	2NT
Pass	3♠ (3)	Pass	4NT (4)
Pass	5♣ (5)	Pass	5♦ (6)
Pass	5♥ (7)	Pass	6♠
All Pass			

1. natural and forcing to 2NT
2. 4th suit game-forcing
3. Strong support in spades

4. RKCB
5. 1 or 4 Key Cards
6. Queen ask
7. I've got the ♠Q and the ♥K

West promptly led the ♣A and another after getting encouragement from East. I ruffed and played ♠A and ♠K confirming a 3-2 break and ending in dummy. I now ruffed the third club, entered dummy with a diamond and ruffed the fourth club high, then entered dummy with the ♥K to draw the last trump and claim twelve tricks.

Although a text-book dummy reversal, I was feeling pretty pleased with myself until score-up when I learned that the opposition had bid the slam and my team mate had led a diamond shortening the play considerably. Sigh, just another flat board.

The next deal was a disaster and prompts the instruction – "Assign the blame".

Dealer South, Both Vulnerable

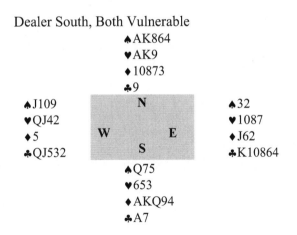

```
                    ♠AK864
                    ♥AK9
                    ♦10873
                    ♣9
    ♠J109            N            ♠32
    ♥QJ42                         ♥1087
    ♦5         W         E        ♦J62
    ♣QJ532           S            ♣K10864
                    ♠Q75
                    ♥653
                    ♦AKQ94
                    ♣A7
```

The bidding went as follows:

WEST	NORTH	EAST	SOUTH
			1NT (1)
Pass	2♥ (2)	Pass	2♠ (3)
Pass	3♦ (4)	Pass	3♠ (5)
Pass	4♠	All Pass	

1. 15-17 hcp
2. Transfer to spades
3. Didn't super-accept, also denying 4 and (in some systems) a minimum
4. Natural suit and game force
5. Strong support in spades

I was South and thought that a 4♥ cue bid by North was a stand-out after the strong 3♠ bid and that the failure to show the heart control denied having it. My partner thought that having bid 3♦ missing the AKQ already showed a strong hand.

Curiously enough, I recently read "another 52 Great Bridge Tips" by David Bird in which one of his tips was not to bid your second suit in a similar sequence unless you were strong and interested in slam – the exact point made by my partner. It's a pity that we didn't co-ordinate our reading habits.

On reflection, I could have just punted 6♦ if I thought there was any doubt about his not showing the heart ace or even after he bid 4♠, but the grand would have been easy if he had have bid 4♥.

The hand was from a tournament divided into Open, Women, Seniors and Juniors. The Bulletin indicated that in the Open field no-one bid the grand, with three pairs in game. In the Women's field, everyone bid to slam with one grand. In the Seniors, most of the pairs were in game with two small slams and the Juniors divided with some in the grand, some in the small slam and some in game.

Is this a commentary about the young and female of the species?

The result was flat in our match, demonstrating that the scores don't show all. Notwithstanding, it was still a disaster.

This deal has a cute play component.

The bidding went as follows:

WEST	NORTH	EAST	SOUTH
		Pass	1♣
Pass	1♦ (1)	Pass	1♥ (2)
Pass	1♠ (3)	Pass	2♠ (4)
Pass	3♥ (5)	Pass	4♥ (6)
Pass	4NT (7)	Pass	5♦ (8)
Pass	6♥	All Pass	

Dealer East, Both Vulnerable

```
                    ♠AK10
                    ♥QJ94
                    ♦AK108
                    ♣J5
        ♠Q942        N         ♠J6
        ♥5                     ♥7632
        ♦QJ65    W     E       ♦97432
        ♣Q964        S         ♣K10
                    ♠8753
                    ♥AK108
                    ♦
                    ♣A8732
```

1. Intending to show strength later
2. Showing a 4441 or 5-4 type shape
3. Artificial game force
4. Completing the description of the hand
5. Setting hearts
6. I've said enough
7. RKCB
8. 0 or 3 Keycards

West led a heart won in the South hand with the ♥10. The A♠ and K♠ were won and two spades in the South hand were pitched on the top two diamonds and a diamond ruffed with the A♥, followed by a club being ducked.

East was on lead (see below) and sent out a second heart preventing the high cross ruff. However, declarer could now play three rounds of hearts ending in the North hand.

This squeezed West in three suits allowing twelve tricks to be made.

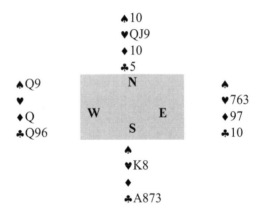

```
                    ♠ 10
                    ♥ QJ9
                    ♦ 10
                    ♣ 5
                        N
  ♠ Q9                             ♠
  ♥                                ♥ 763
  ♦ Q          W           E       ♦ 97
  ♣ Q96                            ♣ 10
                        S
                    ♠
                    ♥ K8
                    ♦
                    ♣ A873
```

This next deal is about hand evaluation. I believe the noted sequence is a good way to get to the sound heart slam.

Dealer West, Both Vulnerable

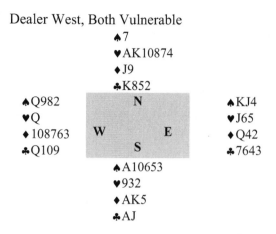

♠7
♥AK10874
♦J9
♣K852

♠Q982   ♠KJ4
♥Q   ♥J65
♦108763   ♦Q42
♣Q109   ♣7643

♠A10653
♥932
♦AK5
♣AJ

WEST	NORTH	EAST	SOUTH
Pass	1♥	Pass	1♠
Pass	2♥	Pass	3♣(1)
Pass	4♣(2)	Pass	5♥ (3)
Pass	6♥(4)	All Pass	

1. Game try with club values
2. Yes I can help clubs
3. Do you have good hearts?
4. Yes.

Of course, South can just bid six (or five asking for good trumps) after the 2♥ response by opener. This equally wins the money, but is not as elegant (as if that counts for anything!).

The next deal is about optimism over bidding technique. I was South and decided that I wanted to get to game with just a modicum from partner despite his original pass, so I opened a game forcing 2♣ in fourth seat.

Dealer West, Both Vulnerable

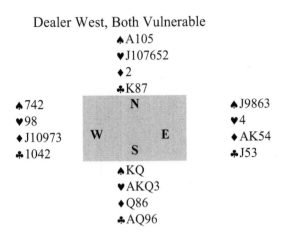

<pre>
                    ♠A105
                    ♥J107652
                    ♦2
                    ♣K87
    ♠742   N   ♠J9863
    ♥98   ♥4
    ♦J10973   W   E   ♦AK54
    ♣1042   S   ♣J53
                    ♠KQ
                    ♥AKQ3
                    ♦Q86
                    ♣AQ96
</pre>

He gave me a positive response of 2♦ (an Ace and a King equivalent), I showed a balanced hand, he transferred to hearts (3♦) and I just bid 6♥.

Of course I was relieved with the singleton diamond. Had I lengthened the auction with cue bids we would have been equally successful by identifying the diamond shortage.

WEST	NORTH	EAST	SOUTH
Pass	Pass	Pass	2♣
Pass	2♦	Pass	2NT
Pass	3♦	Pass	6♥
All Pass			

This was a pick-up against game in the other room.

However, we didn't need to bid blindly or just rely on hope. He should not have been so conservative and should have opened 2♥ showing six hearts and 8-11 points with the bidding as follows resulting in a conclusion offering science over optimism:

WEST	NORTH	EAST	SOUTH
Pass	2♥	Pass	2NT (1)
Pass	3♦ (2)	Pass	4NT (3)
Pass	5♣(4)	Pass	6♥(5)
All Pass			

1. Forcing inquiry
2. Diamond shortage
3. RKCB
4. One key card in hearts
5. Content

The next two deals occurred on the same night – one with a happy ending and the other the reverse. Both times me and partner were just observers with the opposition seemingly quite unwitting in their approaches. See what you think from my spot as West.

Dealer East, North-South Vulnerable

```
                    ♠AKQ
                    ♥AQ10
                    ♦AQJ3
                    ♣K87
      ♠108764          N          ♠J953
      ♥J5                         ♥92
      ♦74          W       E      ♦K1085
      ♣A952            S          ♣Q106
                    ♠2
                    ♥K87643
                    ♦962
                    ♣J43
```

WEST	NORTH	EAST	SOUTH
	2♣ (1)	Pass	2♦ (2)
Pass	2NT (3)	Pass	3♦ (4)
Pass	4♥ (5)	Pass	4NT (6)
Pass	5♦ (7)	Pass	6♥ (8)
All Pass			

1. Game force
2. Negative
3. Big balanced hand
4. Transfer to hearts
5. Showing a very good hand with a heart fit
6. South falls in love with her hand and asks for Key Cards
7. North shows 3 Key Cards
8. South thinks North has 4 Key Cards

What do you think about South asking for Keycards? Somewhat of a role reversal?

Partner leads the ♥2 and I try to signal club preference with the ♥5. I am quite surprised at South's optimism and feel as if we will beat the contract. After a long time of thinking, declarer eventually draws trumps and takes the diamond finesse and trusty partner leads a club for one down.

Afterwards, we all observe with all four hands on view that if instead of playing for the diamond king onside, declarer had played for the club ace onside, then he would have made twelve tricks by pitching two diamonds from dummy using the spades and taking a ruffing finesse in diamonds and using the extra diamond for a later club pitch.

Tough choice for declarer, but one for the good guys since our team mates settle for a boring 4♥ contract making 650.

Contrast the next deal where I was also West.

Dealer West, North-South Vulnerable

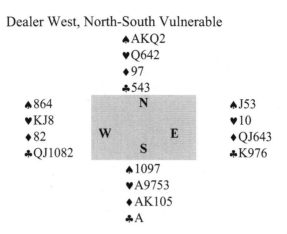

♠AKQ2
♥Q642
♦97
♣543

♠864　　　　　　　　　　　♠J53
♥KJ8　　　　　　　　　　　♥10
♦82　　W　　E　　♦QJ643
♣QJ1082　　　S　　　♣K976

♠1097
♥A9753
♦AK105
♣A

The bidding:

WEST	NORTH	EAST	SOUTH
Pass	Pass	Pass	1♥ (1)
Pass	2♦ (2)	Pass	4♦ (3)
Pass	4♥ (4)	Pass	5♣ (5)
Pass	5♠ (6)	Pass	6♦ (7)
Pass	6♥ (8)	All Pass (9)	

1. Normal so far
2. Agreed by the North-South partnership as being Drury – a good heart raise after passing
3. Assuming North has diamonds and showing a strong hand with hearts and diamonds
4. Hoping that South gets the gag
5. South now cue bids (still for diamonds)
6. North assumes that South knows what is going on and cooperates with a cue that propels the contract to the slam zone
7. South settles for the diamond slam
8. North corrects
9. South passes thinking North has hearts and diamonds and I secretly hope that South has ♥AQ.

As can be seen, twelve tricks are easy with the heart situation and the spades breaking 3-3. South apologises to his partner for forgetting Drury but forgets to apologise to East-West.

Needless to say, no-one else bid this slam. I scratch my head as I leave the table and at least feel happy that the slam breaks were 50:50 tonight. By the way, we won both matches by bidding two successful slams ourselves, so the opposition's ineptitude did shine through eventually.

On this next deal after much consideration, I decided to open 5♣. Since I was vulnerable, partner would know I was serious and act accordingly. As expected she raised to 6♣ with her three fast tricks, trump support and late spade ruffing potential.

I am glad that she didn't consider the grand! The defence was easy on me leading the K♥ so I was able to ruff a spade. Only 6 out of 33 bid this one, so it was a good pick-up on an otherwise less than ideal night.

Dealer South, North-South Vulnerable

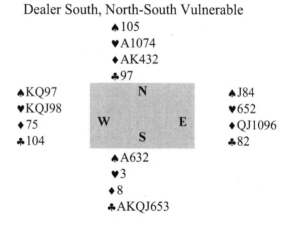

```
                    ♠ 105
                    ♥ A1074
                    ♦ AK432
                    ♣ 97
        ♠ KQ97           N           ♠ J84
        ♥ KQJ98                      ♥ 652
        ♦ 75        W       E        ♦ QJ1096
        ♣ 104           S           ♣ 82
                    ♠ A632
                    ♥ 3
                    ♦ 8
                    ♣ AKQJ653
```

After the game, the result sheets showed that the slam was cold even after a trump lead. I investigated Deep Finesse and found that because West has the sole heart control and East has the sole diamond control, that the hand resolves itself into a simple double squeeze with spades as the pivotal suit.

Say South leads a trump. Declarer then ducks a spade and the defenders then need to return the second trump simultaneously preventing a spade ruff and drawing trumps.

Declarer then plays three rounds of diamonds (pitching a spade and ruffing the third diamond) and runs trumps until something like the following ensues:

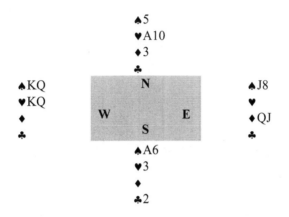

When the last trump is played, West must retain two hearts and so pitches a spade while dummy discards the ♥10. East can spare a diamond at this juncture, but after the ♥A is played, East is squeezed out of a spade and so the A&6♠ are worth two tricks.

Would I have found this line? I prefer to believe that I would, but you can judge for yourselves from experience of my other adventures reported in this chronicle.

It's a new competition, we have a good team and I evaluate our chances as being positive. However, valuations are subjective and not always correct as you will see.

All of the following boards occurred on the same night, cumulatively to my team's detriment.

Against Team A there were several hands of interest.

Example 1:

Dealer North, All Vulnerable

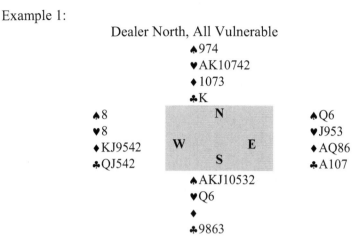

♠974
♥AK10742
♦1073
♣K

♠8
♥8
♦KJ9542
♣QJ542

♠Q6
♥J953
♦AQ86
♣A107

♠AKJ10532
♥Q6
♦
♣9863

My partner North opens 2♥ showing 8-11hcp and six Hearts. After South passes, I bid 4♠ and that's the final contract.

West leads the singleton heart and shortly thereafter I have twelve tricks for plus 680. A perfect fit. I could have bid 2NT asking about singletons and strength, but we are only an occasional pairing so I don't want to have any doubt about what's trumps.

I am not concerned about missing slam and strangely enough, my team mates play 5♦ and return with a plus 620 for a double game swing. This is a big pick-up which I didn't foresee and you would think that bodes well.

Example 2:
First to bid, I consider my options. Not good enough to game force. 2NT is best for hcp description (and is probably the best bid anyway), but I decide to choose a 1♠ bid and hope for more bidding.

My partner responds with a Bergen bid of 3♥ showing 10-11hcp and three spades.

Dealer South, East-West Vulnerable

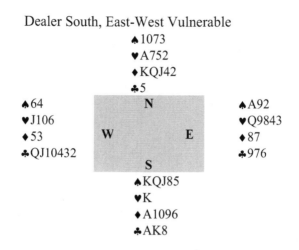

♠1073
♥A752
♦KQJ42
♣5

♠64
♥J106
♦53
♣QJ10432

♠A92
♥Q9843
♦87
♣976

♠KQJ85
♥K
♦A1096
♣AK8

This is a serious under-evaluation and he should have bid 2♦ on the way to a raise by him to 4♠. I think about a variety of hands and settle for 4♠ myself. I haven't come close to describing the strength of my hand.

WEST	NORTH	EAST	SOUTH
			1♠
Pass	3♥	Pass	4♠
All Pass			

While I still think that he is initially at fault, I think I should have bid 4♦ (a long suit trial bid) along the way. Despite him being an occasional partner, this should have prompted a 4♥ cue saying I have the heart ace and diamond help which would then allow me to bid the small slam with some confidence.

This one definitely worries me. A simple twelve tricks and as expected the opposition bid it easily. Bad estimates of value from both me and partner.

Example 3:

Dealer North, All Vulnerable

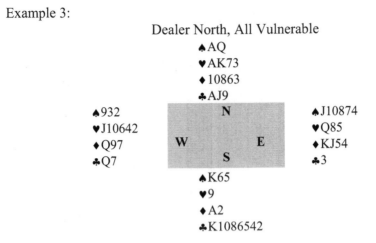

♠AQ
♥AK73
♦10863
♣AJ9

♠932
♥J10642
♦Q97
♣Q7

N
W   E
S

♠J10874
♥Q85
♦KJ54
♣3

♠K65
♥9
♦A2
♣K1086542

The opposition North opens 1♦ and South unhesitatingly bids 2♣. North bids 2♥, a strong reverse (instead of a bid of 3NT which would have shown 18-19hcp with a balanced hand and which better describes the shape).

South bids 3♣ and now North bids 3NT. This could have ended the auction, but no, South bids 4NT (quantitative) and North responds as RKCB with 5♦ showing 0 or 3 KeyCards in clubs.

South mutters about wishing that she knew the system better and resignedly settles in 6♣. I lead a spade and declarer quickly claims thirteen tricks now muttering about missing the grand.

WEST	NORTH	EAST	SOUTH
	1♦	Pass	2♣
Pass	2♥	Pass	3♣
Pass	3NT	Pass	4NT
Pass	5♦	Pass	6♣
All Pass			

I don't think much about it until the score-up when I hear that my team mates bid 1♦-1NT; 3NT for another slam loss. A truly strange evaluation by our international player (as South) to bid 1NT with a 7-card suit and a singleton heart.

Example 4

After East passed, South opened 1♠ and North bid 2♥. South rebid 2♠ and North bid 3♣ with South responding 3♥. RKCB followed, but North strangely subsided in 5♥. Lucky for us since twelve tricks were easy with the 3-3 heart break.

Not a great slam in theory, but great in actuality. I was unreasonably hopeful that my team mates would chance their arm here, but no. They played in 4♥ and we lost an imp on a different defence.

Dealer East, East-West Vulnerable

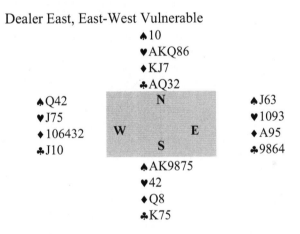

```
                    ♠10
                    ♥AKQ86
                    ♦KJ7
                    ♣AQ32
   ♠Q42                          ♠J63
   ♥J75                          ♥1093
   ♦106432    W         E        ♦A95
   ♣J10            S             ♣9864
                    ♠AK9875
                    ♥42
                    ♦Q8
                    ♣K75
```

So the 14 board match finished and they won the slams by 3:1 which was just about the losing margin. I thought we might recover in the second match, but there were two more slams waiting to test that theory.

Against Team B:

After East passed, I as South opened 1NT. North transferred to diamonds and then showed four spades and I settled for 3NT. The ♣10 lead was ducked to my ♣Q and I cashed ace and king of diamonds and was going to settle for nine tricks, but with the favourable spade layout and some favourable mis-defence, I made twelve tricks. I thought we might gain an imp.

Example 1: Dealer East, All Vulnerable

```
                    ♠AK102
                    ♥6
                    ♦KJ1094
                    ♣J86
     ♠J3              N              ♠97654
     ♥J954                           ♥1082
     ♦53          W       E          ♦Q62
     ♣A10942          S              ♣K5
                    ♠Q8
                    ♥AKQ73
                    ♦A87
                    ♣Q73
```

WEST	NORTH	EAST	SOUTH
		Pass	1NT
Pass	2NT	Pass	3♦
Pass	3♠	Pass	3NT
All Pass			

However, at the other table – South opened 1♥ and North bid 1♠. South then bid 2NT showing 18-19hcp (an upgrade evaluation) and North now bid 3♦. South contented himself with 3NT but North thought otherwise and leapt to 6NT.

WEST	NORTH	EAST	SOUTH
		Pass	1♥
Pass	1♠	Pass	2NT
Pass	3♦	Pass	3NT
Pass	6NT	All Pass	

You would think that was good for us with two quick club tricks for us in a suit not bid by the opposition, but this was not to be. West, an experienced international player, led the 5♦!!!!!
This was unsuccessful and represented a loss of 13 imps and a swing of 26 (more than the difference of the match result).

Finally, Example 2:

Dealer South, All Vulnerable

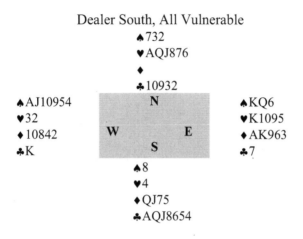

♠732
♥AQJ876
♦
♣10932

♠AJ10954
♥32
♦10842
♣K

♠KQ6
♥K1095
♦AK963
♣7

♠8
♥4
♦QJ75
♣AQJ8654

Partner (South) opened 3♣ and West passed. I jumped to 5♣ and East doubled. West bid 5♠ and without hesitation I bid 6♣. East's double closed the auction.

The ♠A was led and continued. Partner ruffed and quickly played the ♣A and then played for East to have the ♥K. Twelve tricks and plus 1540. While I noted at the table we were playing at that it could be a flat board, I lived in hope.

WEST	NORTH	EAST	SOUTH
		Pass	3♣
Pass	5♣	Double	Pass
5♠	6♣	Double	All Pass

Score-up revealed more hopes dashed. The bidding was identical, but West led a heart. This allowed declarer to play the hand similarly for thirteen tricks and plus 1740 – a 5 imp loss for us.

Thank goodness that night has passed. I will return for more attempts at success, but only after re-assessing my valuation criteria.

Here are a couple of successful bids from a local Pairs event. Would you and your partner have been as successful?

Dealer West, North-South Vulnerable

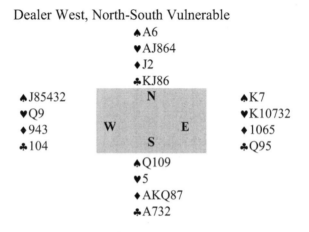

♠A6
♥AJ864
♦J2
♣KJ86

♠J85432
♥Q9
♦943
♣104

♠K7
♥K10732
♦1065
♣Q95

♠Q109
♥5
♦AKQ87
♣A732

After East's pass, I bid 1♦ and partner bid 1♥. I responded 2♣ natural and a one-round force (3♣ would be a splinter) and partner bid 4♣ bringing a quick 6♣ response from me. West led a spade which I won with the ace, played ♣A K followed by diamonds pitching the losing spade.

The defence could only make their high trump.

WEST	NORTH	EAST	SOUTH
		Pass	1♦
Pass	1♥	Pass	2♣
Pass	4♣	Pass	6♣
All Pass			

An easy top in this middling field.

Dealer East, East-West Vulnerable

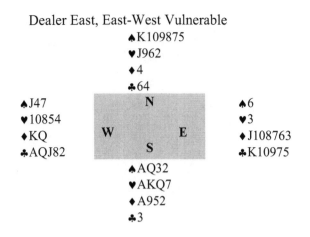

```
                    ♠K109875
                    ♥J962
                    ♦4
                    ♣64
    ♠J47                           ♠6
    ♥10854          N              ♥3
    ♦KQ         W       E          ♦J108763
    ♣AQJ82          S              ♣K10975
                    ♠AQ32
                    ♥AKQ7
                    ♦A952
                    ♣3
```

East passed, partner (South) opened 1♦ and West bid 2♣. I as North
thought about a negative double but decided on bidding 2♠. Partner got
excited and we quickly reached 6♠ despite some additional club
bidding by the opposition. Nothing to the play. Note that 6♥ also
makes. Another victory for the goodies.

We didn't come to grips on the next deal because as a new partnership
we hadn't yet discussed this sequence.

Dealer East, Nil Vulnerable

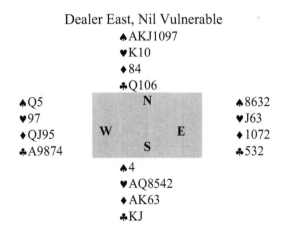

```
                    ♠AKJ1097
                    ♥K10
                    ♦84
                    ♣Q106
    ♠Q5                             ♠8632
    ♥97             N               ♥J63
    ♦QJ95       W       E           ♦1072
    ♣A9874          S               ♣532
                    ♠4
                    ♥AQ8542
                    ♦AK63
                    ♣KJ
```

The bidding went as follows:

WEST	NORTH	EAST	SOUTH
		Pass	1♥
Pass	1♠	Pass	2♦
Pass	3♠	Pass	4♠
All Pass			

Partner thought his 3♠ bid was strong and forcing, while I suggested that he should have bid a game-forcing 3♣ first with his 3♠ bid only showing long spades and an invitational type hand.

Possibly the bidding could have been as follows:

WEST	NORTH	EAST	SOUTH
		Pass	1♥
Pass	1♠	Pass	2♦
Pass	3♣ (1)	Pass	3♥ (2)
Pass	3♠ (3)	Pass	3NT (4)
Pass	4♥ (5)	Pass	4NT (6)
Pass	5♥ (7)	Pass	6♥
All Pass			

1. Artificial game-forcing
2. Extra length in hearts
3. Good spades
4. Club stoppers
5. Heart support
6. RKCB
7. Two Keycards in hearts

With hearts 3-2 the play is easy with no ruffs. An unlikely spade lead from West might give declarer a few palpitations, but twelve tricks should also result. Of course, there are also twelve tricks in NT with no finesses.

Six out of 36 tables bid 6♥ while one table bid 6♠.

So, when playing with a new partner remember to have a broad discussion before you miss a slam.

Time to focus on being declarer and taking control from those other three annoying inhabitants at the table.

4   Chapter 4 – Bidding and Declarer Play

They say that bidding to the right contract takes care of most problems, but declarer play is the most popular part of the game and not only relies on technique and a knowledge of the odds, but also takes advantage of the defenders' lack of sight of their partner's hand.

Here was a deal where I was unaccustomedly successful. The bidding was excessive and informative while the contract was less than secure with four expected losers.

WEST	NORTH	EAST	SOUTH
	1♣	Pass	1♥
2♦	2♥	2♠	3♥
4♣	4♥	All Pass	

Dealer North, Nil Vulnerable

```
                    ♠J984
                    ♥AKQ7
                    ♦74
                    ♣K107
    ♠73               N           ♠KQ1062
    ♥10                           ♥652
    ♦KQ652     W          E       ♦1083
    ♣AQJ84            S           ♣93
                    ♠A5
                    ♥J9843
                    ♦AJ9
                    ♣652
```

The ♠7 was led to the nine, ten and ace. A heart to the ace drew the ♥10 which looked like a singleton.

A finesse of the ♦9 followed which was taken by a tricky ♦K (it certainly tricked East, but not me, as we shall see later).

West gave the deal little further thought when he exited with a spade. The ♣Q instead would have perhaps led to an easier defence for East, but he still had a chance when he won the second spade to find the winning line by leading a second diamond.

Probably influenced by West's earlier diamond deceit, he led a trump won in dummy. A spade ruff followed next with a small club then being played. West played ♣A and ♣Q with the king winning in dummy. The final spade was ruffed and the hearts then run from North squeezing West in clubs and diamonds in the two card ending: North holding ♦4 and ♣10, South ♦AJ and West ♦Q6, ♣J with a card to discard.

It wouldn't have helped if West ducked the first club. The play would have developed the same way and West would have eventually been subject to a throw-in squeeze in this three card ending: North ♦4 and ♣107; South ♦AJ, ♣6 and West ♦Q6, ♣AJ with a card to discard.

Well, that was me and them performing a dummy reversal with squeeze to bring home the bacon. I guess the Beatles knew what they were talking about when they popularised "I'll get by with a little help from my friends". Meanwhile, remember to fool partner only when he can't go wrong.

As I've remarked many times, it's better to be lucky than good. The following hand was published in *Australian Bridge* in the 1970s under the title of the Lucky Expert. On reflection, perhaps only the first word is correct. After two passes, I faced this problem.

N
♠AK653
♥1043
♦QJ
♣632

S
♠J9
♥K7
♦AK1095
♣A1095

As South, I opened 1NT (14-17 hcp) (not the biggest crime) and partner bid 3NT after first transferring to spades.

The fourth best ♣7 is led and draws the two, king and ace. Eight tricks are apparent and the simplest line is to cross to dummy and lead towards the ♥K. This 50% line works if the ace is with East, but is less than satisfactory if not. In any case, running the diamond suit will provide many clues to possible alternative lines without any immediate sacrifice.

On the run of the diamonds, West pitches the ♦2, ♥5, ♠4 and ♥2 and ♥J. These discards should have convinced me to return to the original plan of entering dummy with a spade and leading towards the ♥K, but I obviously had long since forgotten that simple approach and I thought I could draw two of West's spades playing him for 4315 shape.

I thus cashed the ♠A, ♠K and led a club.

Disconcertingly, East followed with the ♣4 and West took the ♣10 with the ♣J. After some thought, West leads the ♠Q with your last four cards being ♥K-7 and ♣9-5. It is a little late for too much more analysis, but you now know that West was 4414 shape and at this point holds the ♠Q (tabled), a heart and Q-8 clubs. If West's heart is the ace, all is good and in any event a club discard is out of the question, so your ♥7 hits the table.

Alas, West cashes the high club and then plays the ♥Q. Congratulations! The momma poppa line would have won and not only that you have engineered a squeeze on declarer with you regrettably still being the declarer!

What's so lucky about this you may well ask? Well, have a look at the complete hand:

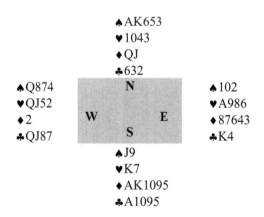

```
                    ♠AK653
                    ♥1043
                    ♦QJ
                    ♣632
   ♠Q874            N              ♠102
   ♥QJ52                           ♥A986
   ♦2        W            E        ♦87643
   ♣QJ87            S              ♣K4
                    ♠J9
                    ♥K7
                    ♦AK1095
                    ♣A1095
```

Naturally, as the Lucky Expert you took particular care with your discards. Here is the four-card ending in which West led the ♠Q, the ♣Q and the ♥Q:

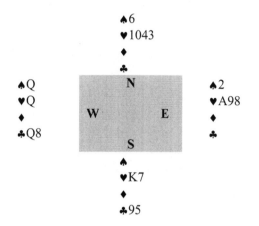

```
                    ♠6
                    ♥1043
                    ♦
                    ♣
        ♠Q           N           ♠2
        ♥Q                       ♥A98
        ♦         W     E        ♦
        ♣Q8                      ♣
                    S
                    ♠
                    ♥K7
                    ♦
                    ♣95
```

No more need for self-recrimination. The ♥10 or the ♣9 generates the ninth trick and you are once again basking in the warmth of success. Aren't happy endings nicer? And isn't my oft-quoted comment at the start of this hand apt?

The following hand (originally reported in *Australian Bridge* in October 1984) was played excellently by my partner at the time (Terry Brown) who still continues to play at international level. He didn't take long to arrive at the best line.

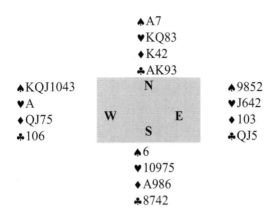

♠A7
♥KQ83
♦K42
♣AK93

♠KQJ1043
♥A
♦QJ75
♣106

♠9852
♥J642
♦103
♣QJ5

♠6
♥10975
♦A986
♣8742

West had opened the bidding with 1 ♠ and East had competed to 2 ♠ over my double (North). I made a further double which enabled Terry to easily bid 4 ♥ as South.

WEST	NORTH	EAST	SOUTH
1 ♠	Double	2 ♠	Pass
Pass	Double	Pass	4 ♥
All Pass			

Against 4 ♥ West led the ♠K. Terry won the ♠A and ruffed the second spade after which he led a heart, West winning with his singleton ace and exiting with the ♣10.

It looks like there are two heart losers and one in each minor, but Terry eliminated that possibility by cashing the two high diamonds and playing a further two rounds of clubs throwing East in with the third club for either a ruff and discard or the loss of the second heart trick. Game made.

This next deal is a contract that a competent declarer should get right, but two declarers warranting that title took far inferior and unsuccessful lines.

Dealer West, All Vulnerable

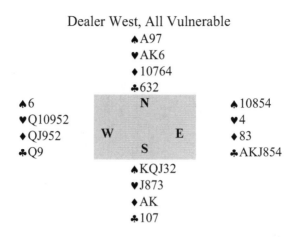

                    ♠A97
                    ♥AK6
                    ♦10764
                    ♣632

    ♠6   N   ♠10854
    ♥Q10952   ♥4
    ♦QJ952   W   E   ♦83
    ♣Q9   S   ♣AKJ854

                    ♠KQJ32
                    ♥J873
                    ♦AK
                    ♣107

Bidding: South became declarer at 4♠ after East showed clubs.
Opening lead: ♣Q

Three rounds of clubs are played and South has to pitch a heart from
hand. East cannot profitably continue clubs allowing another heart pitch
and ruff in dummy, so plays any other suit.

When South draws trumps in four rounds, he finds East with ten cards
in spades and clubs. South can now play the fifth spade squeezing West
in the red suits. This line works for whatever suit East plays at trick
four.

The position after three rounds of clubs, a diamond (say) plus five
rounds of spades (nine cards played) with West having to play a card
and unguard one of the red suits (a simple criss-cross squeeze).

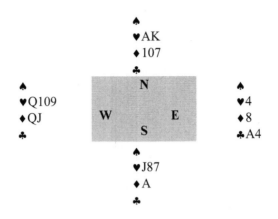

```
            ♠
            ♥AK
            ♦107
            ♣
    ♠              N              ♠
    ♥Q109                         ♥4
    ♦QJ        W        E         ♦8
    ♣                   S         ♣A4
            ♠
            ♥J87
            ♦A
            ♣
```

The following deal was from an Interstate Seniors Team competition held in Hobart, Australia in 2002. Our team mates Ted Griffin and Mike Hughes invariably brought back good results due to their strong all round game. The following hand shows Mike Hughes sitting South as declarer.

Dealer –South, East-West Vulnerable

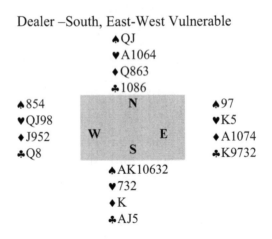

```
                ♠QJ
                ♥A1064
                ♦Q863
                ♣1086
    ♠854              N              ♠97
    ♥QJ98                            ♥K5
    ♦J952       W            E       ♦A1074
    ♣Q8                     S        ♣K9732
                ♠AK10632
                ♥732
                ♦K
                ♣AJ5
```

WEST	NORTH	EAST	SOUTH
			1♣
Pass	1NT	Pass	2♣
Pass	2♦	Pass	4♠
All Pass			

1♣ was 15+, 1NT 9+bal, 2♣ inquiry, 2♦ 9-13, nothing about shape.

After a heart lead, Mike quickly noted that 3NT would have been easier. The ♥Q lead was ducked and a small heart continued to the ace dropping the king. A low diamond from North was won by the ♦K, and a spade played to dummy.

East needed to win the ♦A at this point to set the contract but was worried about a doubleton king in the South hand. A second diamond did not tempt East to fly the ace, but the defensive signals seemed to suggest a 4-4 diamond break.

With this information, Mike led a low club from hand playing for a short honour holding in the West hand. West rose with the queen and in due course, the second spade in dummy served as an entry for the finesse of the ♣K making game against the part score in the other room. If West had ducked (smoothly or otherwise), Mike was going to play the ♣A next anyway.

I got lucky on this next deal where the opposition's bidding was far superior to the declarer play. It was a major event but we were near the bottom of the room, so a little good luck can often come your way.

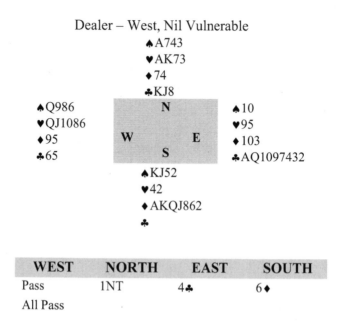

Dealer – West, Nil Vulnerable

```
                    ♠A743
                    ♥AK73
                    ♦74
                    ♣KJ8
    ♠Q986          N            ♠10
    ♥QJ1086                     ♥95
    ♦95       W         E       ♦103
    ♣65           S             ♣AQ1097432
                    ♠KJ52
                    ♥42
                    ♦AKQJ862
                    ♣
```

WEST	NORTH	EAST	SOUTH
Pass	1NT	4♣	6♦
All Pass			

1NT was 15-17hcp.

I as West led the ♣6 and one glance at dummy demonstrated that my hand was a candidate for being squeezed in the majors. All declarer has to do is ruff the first club and play 5 more rounds of diamonds (6 cards in all played). Dummy will hold:

♠A74
♥AK73

West needs to keep 4 hearts and therefore must pitch a spade enabling declarer to set up the third spade and the twelfth trick. It shouldn't have been too hard to imagine that West held the Majors since East had at least 7 to 8 clubs, but as foretold this declarer was overcome with the quality of his bid so failed in his quest for the contract.

Needless to say I was grateful and this gift only just made up for several that my partner had already bestowed on the opposition during the match.

This deal required luck as well as nerve to make up for the overbidding.

Dealer East, All Vulnerable

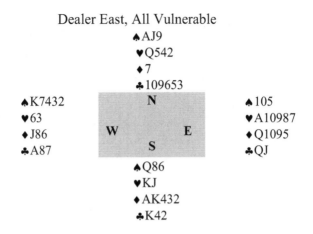

♠AJ9
♥Q542
♦7
♣109653

♠K7432
♥63
♦J86
♣A87

♠105
♥A10987
♦Q1095
♣QJ

♠Q86
♥KJ
♦AK432
♣K42

I as South became declarer in 3NT showing 16-17 points with a 5 card diamond suit. If I recall, partner inquired about a 5 card major in response to my 1NT opening and then decided that 3NT was better than 3♦.

West led the ♠3 followed by the nine, ten and queen of spades. Clubs needed establishing and required a 3-2 break, the ace onside (or if offside, the current magical layout or ace doubleton and extreme foresight by declarer plus two or more rounds of the suit). With all this in mind, I started by leading the ♣2 from hand to the ♣8, 9 and J.

East returned a spade which was won in dummy and the low club continuation drew the ♣Q and ♣A setting up the suit. With East generously holding the ♥A, I made 630 against −130 in the other room for 11 imps in. West can beat the contract by an initial diamond lead, but that of course could not reasonably occur.

This next deal is another example from the playbook of Eddie Kantar's hands where you should "Take All of Your Chances".

Dealer North, Nil Vulnerable

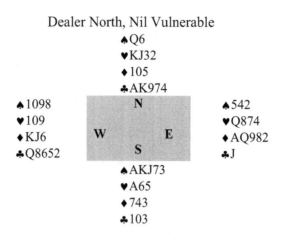

As North I opened 1♣ and East bid 1♦ with partner bidding 1♠. West raised diamonds and eventually South ended up in 4♠.

WEST	NORTH	EAST	SOUTH
	1♣	1♦	1♠
2♦	Pass	Pass	3♦
Pass	3♠	Pass	4♠
All Pass			

West led the ♦K and then sensibly switched to ♠10. After taking the queen in dummy, East can draw trumps and just rely on the heart finesse, but observe the difference if the ♣A is played before a second trump. East per force plays the jack (some would carelessly) say and declarer unblocks the ten. Now after drawing trumps, the odds have swung decisively in favour of the successful club hook, thus ensuring another successful contract without the losing heart hook.

This next deal is similar to the previous example, but I regret to say that neither of the two declarers in our match had absorbed Eddie's advice. The opposition at my table bid to 7♥ while my team mates stopped at 6♥. Both went off two when careful and insightful play produces thirteen tricks.

Dealer North, Nil Vulnerable

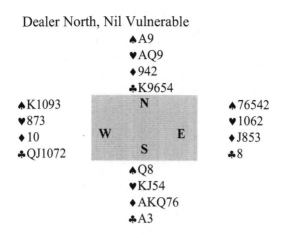

```
                    ♠A9
                    ♥AQ9
                    ♦942
                    ♣K9654
♠K1093          N                ♠76542
♥873                             ♥1062
♦10         W        E           ♦J853
♣QJ1072          S               ♣8
                    ♠Q8
                    ♥KJ54
                    ♦AKQ76
                    ♣A3
```

With only seven hearts, they would be better off in no trumps. Both Easts led the ♣Q.

Assuming diamonds break, there are twelve tricks with a possibility of squeezing West between the clubs and the ♠K (the clubs look certain to be with West).

So, the recommended line is to win the ♣A and cash one high diamond before embarking on trumps. The fall of the ♦10 is a telling card strongly suggesting a singleton (or a clever defender playing from J10x). Then draw three rounds of trumps ending in dummy. The 3-3 break allows you to now lead the ♦9.
Needless to say, you double hook the ♦J8 (restricted choice) and as earlier suggested finish off West for a triumphal claim.

The play of the ♦A at trick two looks to be a no-cost option and can often elicit true count from the defenders or the fall of a key card (as here).

Lucky neither the opposition nor my declarer team mate was up to this, as double success would have been better for the opposition. I have referred both declarers to Eddie K for the future.

I made the following hand with a little help from the opposition by achieving a stepping stone ending which is why it is recorded here. Deep Finesse shows there are many ways to make the hand after the opposition errs at trick three, but this is what actually happened.

Dealer West, East-West Vulnerable

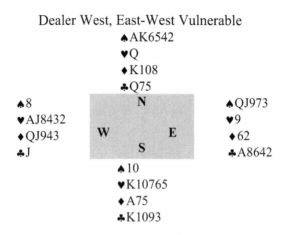

♠AK6542
♥Q
♦K108
♣Q75

♠8
♥AJ8432
♦QJ943
♣J

N
W　　E
S

♠QJ973
♥9
♦62
♣A8642

♠10
♥K10765
♦A75
♣K1093

West opened the bidding with 2♥ showing 6-11hcp and a six-card heart suit. Partner (North) bid 2♠ and East passed. I thought I would show some values with a 2NT bid and partner believed me and raised to game (3NT).

WEST	NORTH	EAST	SOUTH
2♥	2♠	Pass	2NT
Pass	3NT	All Pass	

West led ♥4 and the queen won in dummy clarifying that suit. Not seeing any clear path, I started with a low spade taken by East with the jack.

A diamond return at this point would have spoiled the party (as per Deep Finesse), but East led the ♠7 which I won with the king with West pitching a low heart.

I placed the ♣Q on the table and was pleasantly surprised to see the jack fall as East took the ace identifying West as a 1-6-5-1 shape and presumably with the ♦QJ to give me any chance of success. East led another spade which was won in dummy and the clubs were then run.

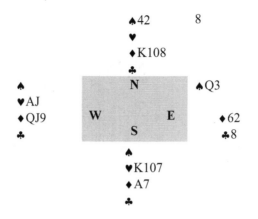

This was the end position after the fourth club with South on lead. I now led a low heart won with the jack. West couldn't cash the other heart so exited with the ♦9 covered with the ♦10. A diamond honour from West would have been fatal. I let the ten win, cashed the ace and threw South in with the ♥A forcing him to give me the ♦K for the ninth trick. I had a lot of fun with this one.

On another regular night at the club, I had erred on the previous board so was looking for a pick-up on this deal. South opened 1♠ (5+ spades) and I as North bid 2♣. South rebid 2NT (usually balanced and not six spades) and after considerable thought I scientifically bid 6NT.

WEST	NORTH	EAST	SOUTH
		Pass	1♠
Pass	2♣	Pass	2NT
Pass	6NT	All Pass	

Dealer South, East-West Vulnerable

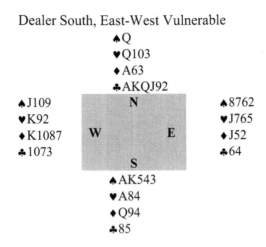

```
                    ♠Q
                    ♥Q103
                    ♦A63
                    ♣AKQJ92
  ♠J109              N              ♠8762
  ♥K92                              ♥J765
  ♦K1087      W           E        ♦J52
  ♣1073                            ♣64
                    S
                    ♠AK543
                    ♥A84
                    ♦Q94
                    ♣85
```

West led the ♠J and partner sat thinking for a long time. Eventually he led the ♣A and West decided to throw the ♣10 to give clear reverse count. Her partner was visibly displeased.

This enabled South to enter his hand with the ♣8 and duck a spade claiming when the spades broke 4-3. My initial impression was that South could enter his hand with the ♥A, play two winning spades stripping West of spades and lead a heart playing West for the king.

This works, but Deep Finesse shows that twelve tricks could be made easily enough (due to West holding both red kings) by leading any of the ♥Q, ♥10, ♥3, ♦6 or♦3 and losing the trick, thus rectifying the count for a subsequent squeeze and throw-in against West which yields twelve tricks.

Anyway, the operation was successful and a pick-up ensued with South being the declarer and the defence unable to cash two quick tricks.

This next deal was irksome. We were playing in a match that we had to win against a team a little ahead of us before the match started. Regrettably, the opposition got everything right and we were the reverse. They quickly bid this to game and the play took no time at all.

Dealer North, North-South Vulnerable

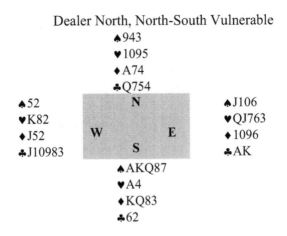

```
                    ♠943
                    ♥1095
                    ♦A74
                    ♣Q754
   ♠52              N              ♠J106
   ♥K82                            ♥QJ763
   ♦J52          W     E           ♦1096
   ♣J10983          S              ♣AK
                    ♠AKQ87
                    ♥A4
                    ♦KQ83
                    ♣62
```

After North passed, East opened 1♥ and South doubled. As West I bid 2♥ and North passed again. South re-opened with 2♠ which North raised to 3♠ (after some thought) and South advanced to 4♠.

WEST	NORTH	EAST	SOUTH
	Pass	1♥	1♠
2♥	Pass	Pass	2♠
Pass	3♠		4♠
All Pass			

Despite the heart lead, South just drew trumps, ducked two clubs (playing for ♣AK bare) and was blessed with a 3-3 diamond split.

Note 3NT has nine tricks with the friendly diamonds and doesn't need the club layout.

This wasn't an actual loss, but typified the trend of the match where things went swimmingly for the opposition who leapfrogged into first position.

There'll be other days.

This was a sad deal where I failed to think about necessary card combinations.

After East passed, I as South decided to open 1♦ planning to rebid spades once or twice later in the auction. West overcalled 2♣, partner passed and East bid 2♥. I now got to bid 2♠ as planned. West leapt to 4♥ and partner came to life with a 4♠ bid that ended the auction.

Dealer East, Nil Vulnerable

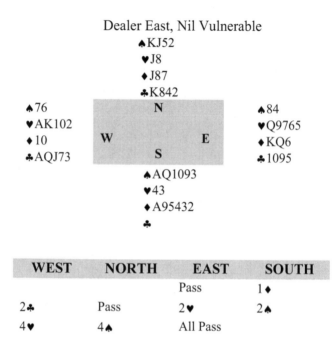

♠KJ52
♥J8
♦J87
♣K842

♠76
♥AK102
♦10
♣AQJ73

♠84
♥Q9765
♦KQ6
♣1095

♠AQ1093
♥43
♦A95432
♣

WEST	NORTH	EAST	SOUTH
		Pass	1♦
2♣	Pass	2♥	2♠
4♥	4♠	All Pass	

West led the ♥A and I could see that the bidding had gone well and that the contract had good chances. West continued with the ♥K followed by the ♣A which I ruffed.

I drew trumps in two rounds and unthinkingly played for a 2-2 break in diamonds. In retrospect, this was a tired and thoughtless approach.

West had shown 11 cards in clubs, hearts and spades and had no room for three diamonds. I needed to address the possibility of a 1-3 break with East holding 3 diamonds. Since a singleton honour with West was of no value, I needed to conclude that the only holding of any interest was a singleton ♦10 with West as was the case.

This required winning the second trump in dummy and playing the ♦J. If East ducks, run the ♦J. If East covers there is only one loser in the suit.

Another chance blown losing the value of the bidding and making me wish that I could stay awake longer.

Note that had I opened with a 1♠ bid, there was always the possibility West may have led his singleton 10 which would have solved the issue without any need for thought by declarer.

I will finish this chapter with a slightly off-beat deal.

I recall reading somewhere that 4-4-4-1 type deals don't always play well, but this example is definitely an exception to that conception.

The bidding reached quite a high level after a very slow start leaving declarer (me) to come up with some sort of justification for this sort of optimism, not based on great trumps, fantastic shape or hcp.

Dealer East – Nil Vulnerable

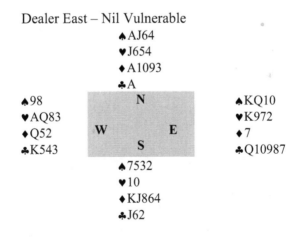

      ♠AJ64
      ♥J654
      ♦A1093
      ♣A

♠98   ♠KQ10
♥AQ83   ♥K972
♦Q52   ♦7
♣K543   ♣Q10987

      ♠7532
      ♥10
      ♦KJ864
      ♣J62

After three passes North started the proceedings with 1♦ which generally shows 4+ diamonds. East had a near ideal takeout double and some fair values for a passed hand and thus had a genuine take-out double.

As South, I bid 1♠ on my meagre collection knowing that I could always fall back to diamonds if North didn't actually have spades. Moreover, I might have been stealing their suit with my ratty spade collection.

West had no trouble entering the fray with a bid of 2♥ and North had no trouble supporting with a bid of 2♠.

East without pause upped the ante with a bid of 3♥ – after all, West had made a free bid over South's bid. As South I thought I had already bid a lot and passed.

At this point, West went into Deep Thought eventually bidding 4♥, although I am not sure of the grounds for this decision. I was pretty happy until I noticed that partner had re-evaluated his shape and strength by taking the push to 4♠.

At least no-one had doubled I mused as West led the ♠9.

WEST	NORTH	EAST	SOUTH
		Pass	Pass
Pass	1♦	Double	1♠
2♥	2♠	3♥	Pass
4♥	4♠	All Pass	

As I considered my 18hcp game contract I took a positive view by noticing the double fit plus the shortages and tried not to focus on the lack of spade pips. I ducked the first spade which East won with the ♠10 and promptly returned the ♠K which I won with the ♠A with East following with the ♠8.

Good news that they broke 3-2.

As all my trumps were effectively equal, I decided to try to ruff a few clubs in dummy and started by cashing the ♣A. Remembering East's take-out double, I unblocked the diamond suit by leading the ♦10 from dummy winning with the ♦A in hand with East significantly playing the ♦7. This allowed me run the ♦6 (finessing West's ♦Q) and remaining in the South hand. It doesn't matter if South covers. I then ruffed a club and started to run the diamonds starting with the ace.

If East had ruffed any of the diamonds, I would then be able to make my remaining trumps separately, so he held off but when they ran out, I ruffed the second club and later made one of two little spades. Making 10 tricks in all.

No-one was more surprised than me. My 1♠ bid was OK as was partner's 4♠ bid plus the cards were kind and I took advantage.

The shibboleths of – don't bid weak suits, don't bid on weak hands without shape and you need say 25 hcp to bid game were all tested and found wanting.

I am still surprised about this deal every time I recall it.

Statistically half of the time you will defend, so you really should practise a bit, preferably keeping partner informed of what you are doing. Let's look at a few examples.

5   Chapter 5 – Successful Defence

If you can improve in this phase of your game, your results will improve substantially. It's like golf, drive for show and putt for dough.

The following hand was originally published in *Australian Bridge* in December 1983.

It's late in the tournament (Pairs) and we do not really seem to be in contention but partner is still very keen. A little bit of application here will be a real confidence builder for this new partner in the coming major events. As usual, partner has passed and your weak jump has not kept them out of game.

WEST	NORTH	EAST	SOUTH
			1♣
2♠ (1)	Double (2)	Pass	4♥ (3)
All Pass			

1. Weak
2. Promising 4 Hearts
3. Ingenuous

You lead the ♠K and observe the following:

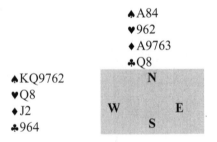

```
              ♠A84
              ♥962
              ♦A9763
              ♣Q8
♠KQ9762           N
♥Q8
♦J2           W        E
♣964              S
```

It is not all gloom though, since declarer appears a little discomforted by his assumed Moysian fit.

After some thought, he wins dummy's ♠A with partner playing the ♠3 and declarer the ♠J, and then declarer follows with a round of hearts, 2 – 4 – 7 and your 8. On lead, you play a second spade on which partner plays the ten and declarer parts with the ♦4. Can you consolidate your apparent early advantage?

There are several clues. Partner's play in spades and declarer's diamond discard suggests a diamond switch. While their combined opinion is

110

almost sufficient justification, let's proceed with the analysis anyway. Declarer's bidding and play suggests a 1-4-3-5 shape with a goodish hand as North's negative double could have been in the 8-9 point range.

Accordingly, partner is unlikely to hold more than 5 points and these should include the ♥J, based on declarer's play of the suit. Hence, it seems best for the defence if partner holds the ♦K instead of the ♣K.

By now, the desire to lead a diamond is overwhelming and happily enough, the defence garners a spade, two hearts and a diamond to set the contract.

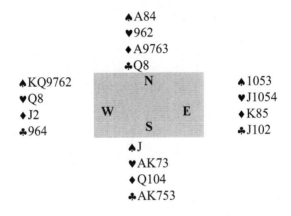

```
                    ♠A84
                    ♥962
                    ♦A9763
                    ♣Q8
      ♠KQ9762          N          ♠1053
      ♥Q8                          ♥J1054
      ♦J2        W         E       ♦K85
      ♣964                 S       ♣J102
                    ♠J
                    ♥AK73
                    ♦Q104
                    ♣AK753
```

The other less thoughtful defence of a third spade would have led to a less pleasant outcome. Declarer would ruff, play off the ♥A and ♥K and run the clubs to reach this position:

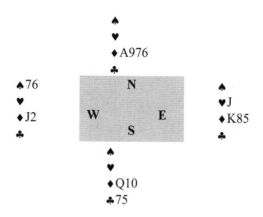

Needing only three more tricks, South keeps leading clubs. East's diamond trick evaporates when East ruffs and has to concede the remaining tricks (an elimination and squeeze forced onto declarer).

Curiously enough, this triumphant defence earned no extra match points since the rest of the field was in either 3NT (making four) or 6♦ also making. Nevertheless, your intangibles (such as reputation, satisfaction and partner's esteem) have been left infrangible.

The following hand was published in *Australian Bridge* in April 1983.

The opponents have been pummelling us and are consequently getting bolder by the minute.

The bidding:

WEST	NORTH	EAST	SOUTH
			1♠
Pass	2♣	Pass	3♠
Pass	4♠	All Pass	

The 3♠ rebid is an Acol 2 equivalent.
They bid yet another game and partner commences play with the two of trumps. Well, are you going to take the insult with the injury or are you going to beat the hell out of this game?

This is what is on sight.

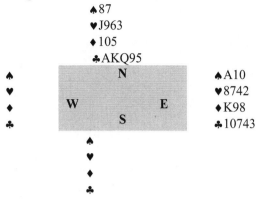

♠87
♥J963
♦105
♣AKQ95

♠A10
♥8742
♦K98
♣10743

If declarer is to be believed, he has eight, or maybe seven, tricks in his hand which, with the three clubs in dummy is enough for game. On this basis, for us to take four tricks before declarer takes ten, partner needs both red suit aces.

But, this would leave too meagre a hand, even for this super-confident declarer. So the only remaining chance is that declarer cannot immediately utilise the club tricks because of a void.

A standard textbook play of the ten of spades ensues allowing you to set the contract with three diamonds and a spade as declarer is unable to take advantage of the favourable heart lie.

Well, you didn't save the match on this board, but at least declarer knows that the next encounter will not be so easy.

The full deal is:

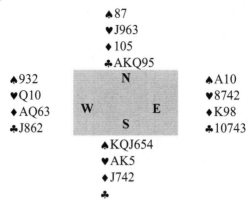

```
                    ♠87
                    ♥J963
                    ♦105
                    ♣AKQ95
  ♠932          N            ♠A10
  ♥Q10                       ♥8742
  ♦AQ63      W     E         ♦K98
  ♣J862          S           ♣10743
                    ♠KQJ654
                    ♥AK5
                    ♦J742
                    ♣
```

Note that if you had have played the ♠A first, that declarer would then succeed with the favourable heart layout

This deal from the 1982 Inter-Cities Tournament in Hong Kong was deceptive, but demonstrated excellent defence based on several switches (reported in *Australian Bridge* October 1982).

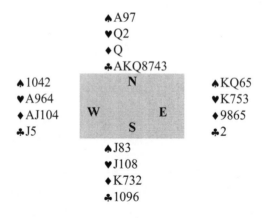

```
                    ♠A97
                    ♥Q2
                    ♦Q
                    ♣AKQ8743
  ♠1042         N            ♠KQ65
  ♥A964                      ♥K753
  ♦AJ104     W     E         ♦9865
  ♣J5            S           ♣2
                    ♠J83
                    ♥J108
                    ♦K732
                    ♣1096
```

At my table, my partner and I bid to 3♣ making ten tricks and were somewhat concerned at missing what appeared to be an easy 3NT. Terry and Margot Brown showed that this cursory analysis deserved re-examination.

The North-South auction, canapé style, went:

WEST	NORTH	EAST	SOUTH
	1♠	Pass	1NT
Pass	3♣	Pass	3♦
Double	3NT	All Pass	

West led the ♥4 to the ♥K and East returned the ♥3 to the ace, setting up declarer's ninth trick. However, having nine tricks is different to taking them.

West continued with a spade to the queen, declarer ducking to retain communications. East punched back a diamond to the ace and another spade was led. Declarer won with the ace but was unable to realise nine tricks when the ♣J failed to drop on the first round.

Good stuff.

This next deal was against an opponent that I love to beat.

Dealer West Nil Vulnerable

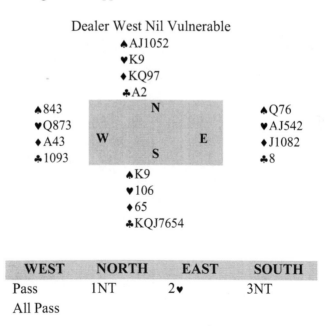

♠AJ1052
♥K9
♦KQ97
♣A2

♠843
♥Q873
♦A43
♣1093

♠Q76
♥AJ542
♦J1082
♣8

♠K9
♥106
♦65
♣KQJ7654

WEST	NORTH	EAST	SOUTH
Pass	1NT	2♥	3NT
All Pass			

115

North (my adversary) opened 1NT (15-17) despite his shape. My partner (Tom Moss as East) bid 2♥ showing 5+ hearts and a 4+ minor. South tanked a while and decided on 3NT which became the final contract although I fleetingly (and foolishly) considered bidding 4♥ as a save.

Partner now played impeccably by leading the ♦2. I won the ace and placed the ♥Q firmly on the table. Partner's ace covered the king and his jack followed. I carefully unblocked the ♥7 and declarer followed with the nine.

With trust (and hope) partner led his ♥2 and we were able to take the contract two off.

Note that on any other lead, the dreaded opponent gets the last laugh. Naturally there were no congratulations from North for the defence, just the regular criticism of his partner's poor choice of bid.

How sweet it was.

This next one is tough but still possible to get right. It is nil vulnerable and partner (East) opens 3♥. South bids 3♠, you bid 4♥ and North pushes on to 4♠. After some thought you double. First you need to lead. Eventually you lead the ♥A and it wins – so far so good but what now with the following in sight?

WEST	NORTH	EAST	SOUTH
		3♥	3♠
4♥	4♠	Pass	Pass
Double	All Pass		

Dealer East, Nil Vulnerable

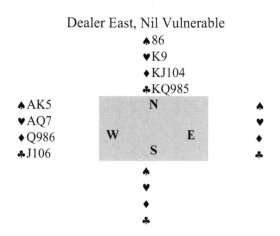

It's possible that partner has an ace although that doesn't leave South with much. Anyway the ♣A is unlikely to need cashing now, so you try a diamond.

The ♦J wins in dummy with East playing the ♦3 and South the ♦2. Partner normally gives reverse count so he has one or two diamonds. The ♠6 is led to the ♠9 with partner following with the ♠2.

You persist with diamonds on the basis that South had some values for his bid and partner ruffs for one down. Partner pre-empted with junk, but your defence saved the day. Hooray! The full hand:

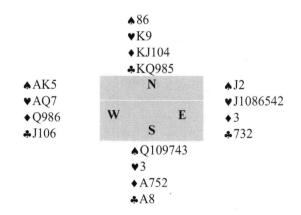

This next one is not that tough, but requires some thought at the table. North as dealer opened 1♦ and South bid 1♠. North then raised to 3♠ and South bid the fourth with East-West silent. Partner leads the ♦6 and this is what you see:

Dealer North, Both Vulnerable

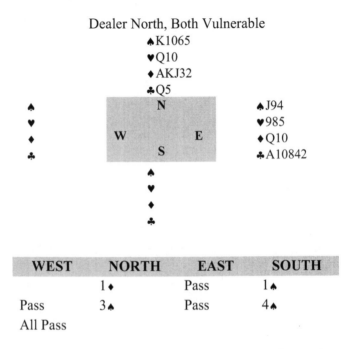

```
                  ♠K1065
                  ♥Q10
                  ♦AKJ32
                  ♣Q5
        ♠                        ♠J94
        ♥          N             ♥985
        ♦      W       E         ♦Q10
        ♣          S             ♣A10842
                  ♠
                  ♥
                  ♦
                  ♣
```

WEST	NORTH	EAST	SOUTH
	1♦	Pass	1♠
Pass	3♠	Pass	4♠
All Pass			

You just follow suit and watch and count as declarer wins the ace in dummy and then plays the ♠A and ♠K with partner playing the ♠7 and ♠Q. Declarer then plays the ♦K dropping your ♦Q while partner plays the ♦4 consistent with a doubleton.

Declarer plays a small diamond to her nine and partner shows either four clubs or values in clubs – depending on your signalling methods (reverse count or reverse attitude) by playing the ♣3. A fourth diamond is led which you ruff as declarer follows and partner discards either the ♥6 (reverse count showing an odd number) or ♥3 (reverse attitude showing values in hearts).

So, you know that declarer is 4-4 in spades and diamonds and wants to use the fifth diamond for a pitch. If you are playing reverse count, then declarer is 4-3-4-2. If reverse attitude then partner has some values in both clubs and hearts. Obviously you need three quick tricks, so what do you do?

The answer is that you need to take your tricks and in the right order. Lead a low club! Partner wins the king and returns a club to your ace and then and only then do you lead a heart.

Having cashed the two clubs, the heart loser can't go away.

However, if you cash ♣A first and continue clubs, then partner will be end-played. Alternatively, if after cashing the ♣A, you switch to a heart, then declarer can win the ♥A and cross to the dummy in spades and pitch a losing club on the fifth diamond.

The full hand:

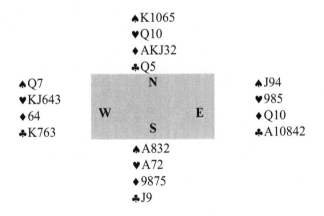

```
                ♠K1065
                ♥Q10
                ♦AKJ32
                ♣Q5
    ♠Q7            N            ♠J94
    ♥KJ643                      ♥985
    ♦64        W       E        ♦Q10
    ♣K763          S            ♣A10842
                ♠A832
                ♥A72
                ♦9875
                ♣J9
```

It seems a bit strange to underlead your club ace, but that's what was necessary. About half of the field made 4♠, which shows either a poor field, or a challenging defence.

I am sure that you as the reader would have got it right when faced with the challenge.

This next one was all over in a flash at our table. I as South bid 1NT and West bid 2♥ showing hearts and another. Partner simply bid 3NT which ended the auction.

East led the ♦J and I confidently played the ♦Q while passively thanking dummy for his contribution. A club finesse followed and West said as he played the ♦A and the other setting diamond tricks that East had shown an even number of cards – one down.

Dealer South, Both Vulnerable

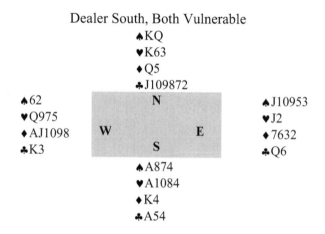

```
                    ♠KQ
                    ♥K63
                    ♦Q5
                    ♣J109872
    ♠62               N              ♠J10953
    ♥Q975                            ♥J2
    ♦AJ1098      W         E         ♦7632
    ♣K3               S              ♣Q6
                    ♠A874
                    ♥A1084
                    ♦K4
                    ♣A54
```

I asked my team mates what lead they got that allowed eleven tricks against them and they said the same with the peremptory comment that there was nothing they could do about it with East indicating attitude on the diamond lead.

A case for better signalling methods or perhaps better partners?

You hold the following hand as West with All Vulnerable and need to find the killing lead.

```
        ♠QJ943
        ♥KQ8
        ♦J4
        ♣964
```

The bidding has been a little strange but that's not what should be occupying your mind right now.

WEST	NORTH	EAST	SOUTH
		1♣	1♥
1♠	Pass	2♣	2♥
Pass	3♥	Pass	4♥
All Pass			

The full hand:

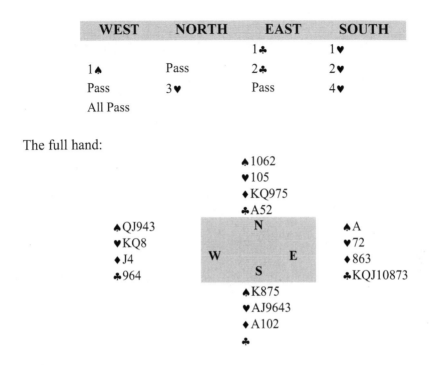

```
                    ♠1062
                    ♥105
                    ♦KQ975
                    ♣A52
      ♠QJ943          N          ♠A
      ♥KQ8                        ♥72
      ♦J4        W         E      ♦863
      ♣964           S            ♣KQJ10873
                    ♠K875
                    ♥AJ9643
                    ♦A102
                    ♣
```

West led a club (his partner's suit) and shortly thereafter declarer had gained 10 tricks and the vulnerable game, losing just two hearts and a spade via drawing trumps.

However, the game can be defeated with a low spade lead (4th best of your longest and strongest the wise men used to say). This changes the timing and allows West to establish a second spade trick before trumps are drawn. Note that the more common lead of a high spade from West initially doesn't work (see later).

I was North on this hand and judged that partner's vulnerable 2♥ bid suggested good playing strength and thus my raise on a doubleton.

A happy ending for me and partner and an interesting but obscure defensive opportunity not taken by the opposition. Of course, not leading your partner's suit has to be justified by success in your alternate choice.

This deal also featured in Ron Klinger's daily newspaper feature in Sydney where West led the ♠Q to the ♠A, after which East led the ♣10. Klinger noted the need for declarer to play ♥A and another heart after this defence to avoid a spade ruff by East.

This deal is tactically interesting.

Dealer East, North-South Vulnerable

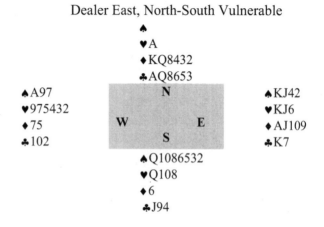

```
                        ♠
                        ♥A
                        ♦KQ8432
                        ♣AQ8653
        ♠A97                N              ♠KJ42
        ♥975432                            ♥KJ6
        ♦75             W       E          ♦AJ109
        ♣102                S              ♣K7
                        ♠Q1086532
                        ♥Q108
                        ♦6
                        ♣J94
```

The bidding:

WEST	NORTH	EAST	SOUTH
		1NT	Pass
2♦	4NT	Pass	5♣
Pass	Pass	Dble	All Pass

East's 1NT was 15-17hcp and West's 2♦ was a transfer to hearts.

North (an Australian International player) showed a strong hand with the minors and South after an interminable time chose her better minor. Even after the hand was over no-one knows what she was thinking about.

In the meantime, partner felt he had to double.

A trump lead by West defeated the contract since the defence not only won the ♣K but was able to draw two trumps eventually winning two diamonds and a club. This was not a hard lead to find due to the revealing bidding.

The interesting thing about the hand is that 5♣ by North can't be beaten since East can't lead trumps without losing his ♣K.

This happy outcome could have been achieved by North bidding 3♦ over the transfer bid with the plan to later bid clubs at the five level thus placing the contract in the right hand. It is difficult to conceive that the 3♦ bid would be passed out.

Ron Klinger wrote about this hand in his daily newspaper column in Sydney and the following bidding occurred at his table.

WEST	NORTH	EAST	SOUTH
		1NT	Pass
2♦	Double	2♥	2♠
3♥	4♣	Pass	5♣
All Pass			

North's first double showed diamonds and later North was able to show a strong hand with diamonds and clubs enabling South to bid the club game.

Klinger also noted that North needed to ruff the second diamond low and the third diamond with the ♣J, finally playing West for either ♣Kx or ♣Kxx and not ♣ K10x.

Food for thought?

Up till now I have covered well known headings, but the last chapter is really out there in a galaxy far, far away. I have included these hands to show that there is always something there to surprise us, even though you aren't expected to get it right at the table.

6   Chapter 6 – Exotica

The hands here serve no purpose apart from confirming that bridge is a difficult game full of complexities.

You hold the following hand as West with North-South vulnerable. It is a Pairs event and the opposition is not top drawer. You hold:

Dealer West, North-South Vulnerable

$\spadesuit$ K82
$\heartsuit$ 92
$\diamondsuit$ AK1073
$\clubsuit$ 1042

You passed initially and North opened 1$\diamondsuit$, partner bids 2$\spadesuit$ (weak jump) and South bids 3$\heartsuit$. You have no trouble raising to 3$\spadesuit$, while North and partner (East) pass leaving South to bid 4$\heartsuit$ which become the final contract.

WEST	NORTH	EAST	SOUTH
Pass	1$\diamondsuit$	2$\spadesuit$	3$\heartsuit$
3$\spadesuit$	Pass	Pass	4$\heartsuit$
All Pass			

Imagine it is left in and it is your lead.

A heart lead is out of the question and declarer sounds long enough in hearts to withstand a spade force, so you consider your diamond holding, but worried by North's opening bid, you reconsider and decide upon the unbid suit, clubs.

Not being sure that you want it returned, you choose the 4$\clubsuit$.

The full hand is:

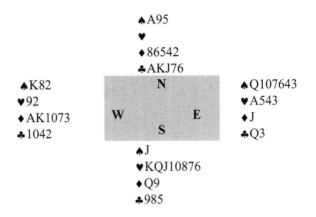

♠A95
♥
♦86542
♣AKJ76

♠K82
♥92
♦AK1073
♣1042

N
W   E
S

♠Q107643
♥A543
♦J
♣Q3

♠J
♥KQJ10876
♦Q9
♣985

Declarer wins in dummy, plays A♠ and ruffs the second spade to get to hand and leads the trump king. Partner wins the ace, returns his singleton diamond and on your second diamond pitches a club whereupon you give him a club ruff for one down.

You have found the lead of the year and a memory for your exotica handbook. Only a club lead will do, assuming declarer reads cards as well as you.

Spoiler alert – you are woken from your moment in the sun by partner announcing he was going to save in 4♠ since he can't rely on you to find the right lead, but even partner was not to get his wish as North himself wants to be a hero and has bid 5♣ ahead of partner.

Indifferent declarer play sees declarer drift three off for a better score than defeating 4♥, but your chance for stardom has come and gone.

On this particular night you have just been beaten up by a respectable pair in a Teams scoring event although a better lead from partner on one hand could have softened the blow. Partners – can't live with them, can't live without them – sound familiar?

Still smarting, you examine the following board which says on the 'hands sheet' should be held to 2NT. North bid a weak 2♠ and South bid a snappy 3NT. Partner naturally as West led the ♣3 and declarer won and continued with the club suit eventually claiming nine tricks with East being squeezed on the clubs.

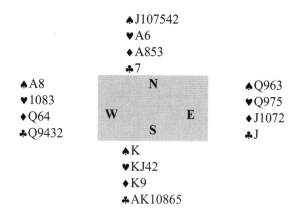

```
              ♠J107542
              ♥A6
              ♦A853
              ♣7
  ♠A8            N         ♠Q963
  ♥1083                    ♥Q975
  ♦Q64       W       E     ♦J1072
  ♣Q9432         S         ♣J
              ♠K
              ♥KJ42
              ♦K9
              ♣AK10865
```

A period of study by me after the match suggests that a low diamond lead may be the solution that eluded partner at the time, but my consultant "Deep Finesse (DF)" says that only the ♦Q will be successful.

I quiz DF some more and on a low diamond lead, South wins and plays two high clubs followed by the ♠K. West needs to unblock the ♦Q but can't get back in before West sets up spades (or four heart tricks).

The lead of the ♦Q unblocks the suit immediately and leads to the situation where declarer is endplayed to concede five tricks. This is a difficult hand even with the aid of DF.
While theoretically partner had a one in thirteen chance of getting this one right, I don't hold him liable for this one and instead the hand just gets filed under Exotica while the opposition leave even happier.

I held the following hand and felt good about it.

```
              ♠K
              ♥AKQJ63
              ♦KQJ
              ♣KQ2
```

I opened a game force 2♣ and after receiving a positive response (2♦), showed my hearts, heard about partner's 5-card club suit, Roman key carded in clubs knowing that if there was only one ace, I could sign off in 5♥, but discovered two aces and confidently bid 6♥.

The bidding:

WEST	NORTH	EAST	SOUTH
			2♣
	2♦	Pass	2♥
Pass	3♣	Pass	4NT
Pass	5♥	Pass	6♥
All Pass			

West led the ♣3 which suspiciously looked like a singleton. Dummy tracked and I was still very pleased.

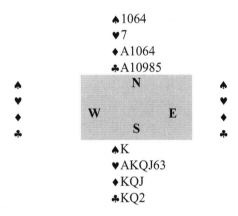

Although I put in the ♣8, East withheld the jack (still assuming the singleton lead).

At this stage I was contemplating making thirteen tricks but upon starting drawing trumps I received a setback with East holding five to the 10♥, posing the question "when is a suit solid?"

Seeing another chance, I drew four rounds of hearts and then found East with the expected four clubs enabling me to set up the fifth club for a spade pitch, thus making the hand.

However, when I flamboyantly played the ♦K overtaking with the ace, East trumped both diamond honours and returned a spade for one off.

The full hand was:

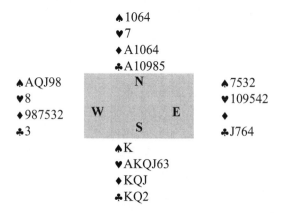

Note the importance of East withholding the ♣J which if played would allow a pitch of the ♠K on the fourth round of clubs.

After recovering from the shock and letdown of the distribution, I noticed that I was very lucky that East had not thrown in a Lightner double.

That would have resulted in down two doubled (-500) instead of the -100 on the scoresheet. So having absorbed this information I could return to my original happy state.

Talking about "when is a suit solid?" this hand turned up recently. I held:

♠AKJ4
♥KQ
♦AKQJ94
♣10

I opened 2♣ (game-force) and partner bid 3♥ which was a semi-positive – i.e. 5 hearts and less than an ace and a king or three kings.

Because we play RKCB as 1430, I was able to Blackwood since a 5♦ response by partner would show no aces and would allow us to settle in that denomination. However, partner bid 5♣ showing one ace and I bid 6♦ which partner respectfully passed.

WEST	NORTH	EAST	SOUTH
			2♣
Pass	3♥	Pass	4NT
Pass	5♣	Pass	6♦
All Pass			

West led the ♠3 and this is what I saw in dummy:

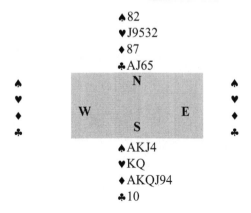

♠82
♥J9532
♦87
♣AJ65

♠AKJ4
♥KQ
♦AKQJ94
♣10

131

I was very pleased. This time my six-card suit had the nine instead of the 6 and partner had two trumps instead of one. I won the ♠J, cashed the ♠A and ruffed a spade which passed without trouble. I then triumphantly stated I would draw enough trumps before giving up a heart.

Alas, West had five diamonds to the ten plus the ♥A and my triumph turned to dust. Since many others were in 3NT making, -50 was not a good score. My concept of a solid suit was once again challenged.

Dealer North – North-South Vulnerable
As South, you hold

♠Q8765432
♥
♦QJ96
♣K

Your partner opens a Multi 2D showing either a six-card major 6-10 hcp or a balanced 23-24 hcp hand. East passes. If partner has the weak two in hearts, then you should bid 2♠ now and later 4♠ which he shouldn't misinterpret.

However after West passes your 2♠ bid, partner shows the big hand and you start to think about specific key cards and bidding sequences, but it all is just too hard and you bash 6♠.

WEST	NORTH	EAST	SOUTH
	2♦		2♠
Pass	2NT	Pass	6♠
All Pass			

132

East leads the ♣2 and you see:

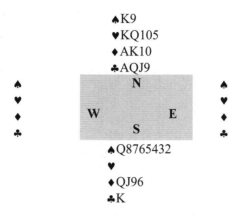

```
              ♠K9
              ♥KQ105
              ♦AK10
              ♣AQJ9
        ♠           N           ♠
        ♥                       ♥
        ♦      W         E      ♦
        ♣           S           ♣
              ♠Q8765432
              ♥
              ♦QJ96
              ♣K
```

You win with the ♣K. Life is good and boldness has been rewarded until you lead a small spade, West inserting the ten, you covering with the K♠ and East shows out!!! Just another kick in the guts by the computer.

Have a look at the East hand to get some idea of the devious computer-generated dealer program. Not everyone is in slam, so the score is less than average. Also you may feel that West was a wee bit timorous. Oh well, on to the next hand.

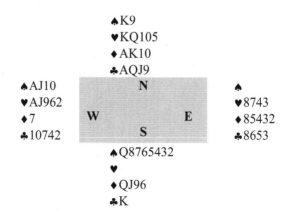

```
                    ♠K9
                    ♥KQ105
                    ♦AK10
                    ♣AQJ9
        ♠AJ10           N           ♠
        ♥AJ962                      ♥8743
        ♦7        W         E       ♦85432
        ♣10742         S           ♣8653
                    ♠Q8765432
                    ♥
                    ♦QJ96
                    ♣K
```

The following short hand was reported in *Australian Bridge* in June 1984.

In an advanced stage of a prestigious teams event, two Sydney teams of good repute encounter. Seven of the eight contestants are regular and familiar rubber bridge players and I am there too. I sense a certain cavalier attitude prevailing. "Now witness the following and know that it truly happened."

Dealer South, East-West Vulnerable

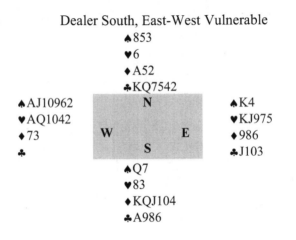

```
                    ♠853
                    ♥6
                    ♦A52
                    ♣KQ7542
    ♠AJ10962                       ♠K4
    ♥AQ1042                        ♥KJ975
    ♦73                            ♦986
    ♣                              ♣J103
                    ♠Q7
                    ♥83
                    ♦KQJ104
                    ♣A986
```

Case 1

WEST	NORTH	EAST	SOUTH
			1♦
1♠ (1)	Pass (2)	Pass	2♣ (3)
2♥	5♣	5♥	Pass
Pass	Double (4)	All Pass	

Lead ♣K (5)
1. With Michaels, Roman Jumps and takeout double available, West chooses to overcall 1♠ . This bid maximises the chance of becoming declarer, whereas the other three bids are distinctly anti-percentage
2. Playing negative doubles and 2♣ as game force
3. Unable to work out who holds the hearts if it is neither partner nor himself!

4. Loaded with defence!

5. A new way to lead top of nothing.

East-West plus 1250

Case 2

WEST	NORTH	EAST	SOUTH
			1♦
1♠ (1)	4♣ (2)	Pass	Pass (3)
4♥ (4)	Double (5)	Pass (6)	All Pass

Lead ♣K (7)

1. With no more than a takeout double available to show the majors, the 1♠ bid is using the creep-up-on-them approach.

2. Probably what he would have bid first in hand. I think it should be filed under C for charisma

3. Showing an acute awareness of partner's bidding tendencies

4. (See 1)

5. Gotcha!

6. Thinking of redoubling

7. Possibly the most reasonable of North's actions to this point

East-West plus 1390

Net to East-West here: +140, 4 imps

Well, 2640 points later, we have picked up 4 imps. I review the lost horizons and note the contracts of –

(a) 1♠ by West (+200 to plus 260)

(b) 5♥ by West (+650 to +710)

(c) 6♣ by N or S doubled (-300)

or even (d) 6♥ by West doubled (-200 to + 1860) were all possibilities. I get my first real taste of rubber(y) bridge.

It was some months after the event that my nerves were sufficiently calmed that I could chronicle the happenings. As I wrote the article, I made a mental note to learn more about this strange form of bridge, but only to achieve observer status.

This hand is more of a bidding problem but, regardless, sits in the Exotica chapter.

Dealer South, East-West Vulnerable

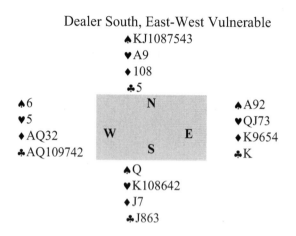

♠ KJ1087543
♥ A9
♦ 108
♣ 5

♠ 6
♥ 5
♦ AQ32
♣ AQ109742

♠ A92
♥ QJ73
♦ K9654
♣ K

♠ Q
♥ K108642
♦ J7
♣ J863

South opened 2♦ multi showing a weak two in one of the majors or a balanced 20-22hcp hand. What should West bid – 3, 4 or 5♣? At the time, I settled for 3♣ although later I thought 4♣ was better. In fact, bidding 3♣ was beneficial as North leapt to 4♠ and partner doubled, passed by South.

The bidding indicated that North had a very long spade suit, South had a weak two in Hearts and partner had some points. This knowledge can now allow an easy 4NT by my hand – asking partner to choose between my long clubs or shorter diamonds (either bid 5♣ or if you have a diamond suit to go with my shorter second suit, bid diamonds) at an appropriate level. Here partner could confidently bid 6♦.
In reality, only 2/18 pairs actually got to diamonds and only at the five level, suggesting that the bidding at other tables wasn't so illuminating.

Needless to say, our score was one of the uneducated 16. Another case of failing to have the confidence of your convictions.

We all have bidding gadgets. One of my current defences to a strong 1NT opening is that a double shows 4 of a major and 5 of a minor. It worked really well on the hand below.

Dealer W, East-West Vulnerable

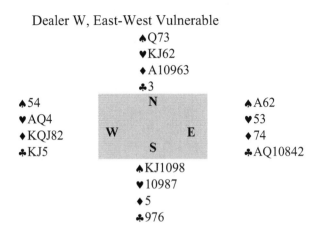

     ♠Q73
     ♥KJ62
     ♦A10963
     ♣3

♠54   **N**   ♠A62
♥AQ4   ♥53
♦KQJ82 **W**   **E** ♦74
♣KJ5   **S**   ♣AQ10842

     ♠KJ1098
     ♥10987
     ♦5
     ♣976

West opened a 15-17 1NT. If I as North passed, East would bid 3NT and I wouldn't be documenting the hand.

Instead, I doubled, East re-doubled (he could still bid 3NT and it wouldn't affect the story) and esteemed partner bid 4♥ which I assumed was pass or correct.

It was then doubled by West.

WEST	NORTH	EAST	SOUTH
1NT	Double	Redouble	4♥
Double	All Pass		

West led the ♣K followed by the ♦K. Partner won the ♦A and led a spade to the Jack followed by the ♥10.

West rose with the ace and got a spade ruff for -100 for us which was a lot better than -600 on any lead. Just the hand for promoting the method, don'cha think?

Of course the bid isn't always suitable and you should stick to your own methods rather than believing me.

WHAT DO YOU BID?
You North, hold with Dealer South, All Vulnerable

♠92
♥AJ10
♦AKQ43
♣843

Partner (me) opens 3♠ vulnerable in first seat showing seven tricks in spades. You have a possible four tricks, but maybe 4 losers. So what to do – game or slam?

I expect you bid 4♠ allowing for the first in hand pre-empt?

The full deal:

Dealer South, All Vulnerable

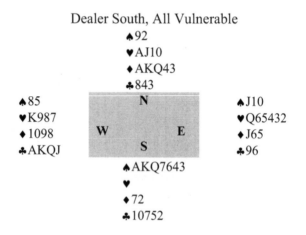

```
                    ♠92
                    ♥AJ10
                    ♦AKQ43
                    ♣843
        ♠85            N            ♠J10
        ♥K987                       ♥Q65432
        ♦1098      W       E        ♦J65
        ♣AKQJ          S            ♣96
                    ♠AKQ7643
                    ♥
                    ♦72
                    ♣10752
```

Yes, it's the old 3NT trick. Don't worry about the weak clubs and the possible lack of access to partner's spades.

The field bid 4♠ and went down after three club tricks and a ruff, but the East at our table had other ideas (it was after all the last board of 180) and he prematurely ruffed the third club trying for a trump promotion.

Unfortunately my hand was the one promoted, again showing how it is possible to make new mistakes nearly anytime. I was grateful to receive.

Against the same pair as on the previous deal, this one came up earlier.

This hand had novelty value in the bidding which went some way to offset the deficiencies in the outcome.

Dealer E, East-West Vulnerable

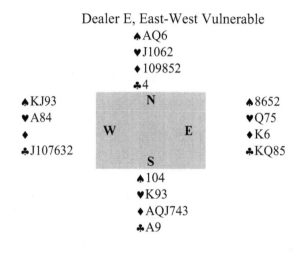

The bidding:

WEST	NORTH	EAST	SOUTH
		1♦ (1)	2♦ (2)
3♦ (3)	4♦ (4)	All Pass	

(1) East-West were playing a complex system where 1♦ showed 8-12hcp and 4 spades.
(2) I bid the suit I had
(3) West showed a splinter, spade support and invitational values
(4) Partner carried away by the novelty of the sequence, thought a part score was enough

So, we had a bidding sequence where everyone made one bid of the same suit!!!

We should have continued the fun by bidding 5♦, then 6♦, but that would have been another story.

Our failure to reach slam was a pick-up with partners making 170 in 2♠ at their table.

While I am pleased to have been present for the auction, I called for a post-match meeting with partner to discuss how to bid 21hcp slams. The match results show only 7 out of 47 tables got to the diamond game, but this doesn't make me feel better.

This hand also had novelty value in the bidding demonstrating that there are different ways to get to the right contract.

Dealer East, Nil Vulnerable

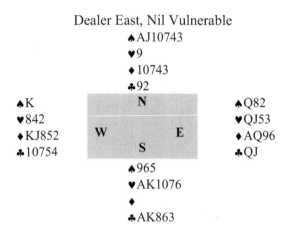

♠AJ10743
♥9
♦10743
♣92

♠K   ♠Q82
♥842   ♥QJ53
♦KJ852   ♦AQ96
♣10754   ♣QJ

♠965
♥AK1076
♦
♣AK863

The bidding:

WEST	NORTH	EAST	SOUTH
		1♦	2NT (1)
3♦ (2)	Pass	Pass	3♠ (3)
Pass	4♠ (4)	All Pass	

1. I as North was playing with a strange partner, but I (correctly) alerted this bid as showing hearts and clubs.
2. Pre-emptive
3. Great idea!
4. I assumed that South had a strong hand with a spade fragment so bid

140

what was likely the best game.

After I raised his fragment, my strange partner glared at me but decided to get out early before further trouble ensued.

West led a diamond and after I put dummy down, the glare turned to a sweet smile with eleven tricks resulting. Half of the field bid it presumably after South made a take-out double.

I was pleased with turn of events and felt "quite nice really".

This next deal was just weird. Partner is usually a very conservative bidder but here emerged from his shell with imagination. East opened a weak 2♠, partner (South passed) and West pre-empted to 3♠. I as North should have bid (probably 3NT) but in tempo subsided with a pass. After East passed, partner (Tom Moss) emerged with a 4♥ bid which ended the auction.

WEST	NORTH	EAST	SOUTH
		2♠	Pass
3♠	Pass	Pass	4♥
All Pass			

Dealer East, East-West Vulnerable

```
                  ♠A95
                  ♥72
                  ♦KQJ3
                  ♣AJ86
    ♠J1074          N           ♠KQ8632
    ♥AK                          ♥J86
    ♦84        W       E         ♦962
    ♣Q9753          S            ♣10
                  ♠
                  ♥Q109543
                  ♦A1075
                  ♣K42
```

Partner was very pleased with dummy and there was no trouble in the play. We had a pick-up with our partners sacrificing in 4♠ doubled for one off.

This deal featured a surprise bid at the four level from a renowned underbidder (which probably stunned the opposition or maybe they thought they were onto a winner) and a vulnerable vs. not sacrifice by our team mates.

Whichever way you look at it, it was sure strange and at the same time quite successful.

WHAT DO YOU BID?

Sitting East, you hold with Dealer West, Nil Vulnerable

♠ 10
♥ 874
♦ KJ86
♣ Q6543

Partner (me as West) opens 1♣ in first seat showing at least three clubs. North pre-empts with 3♦ and you and South pass just to hear a re-opening double from partner. So what to do? It looks pretty obvious – you pass and collect 500 in defence. Wrong!

WEST	NORTH	EAST	SOUTH
1♣	3♦	Pass	Pass
Double	All Pass		

The full deal:

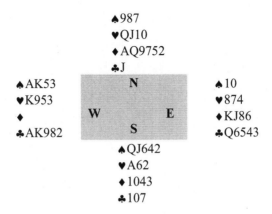

```
            ♠987
            ♥QJ10
            ♦AQ9752
            ♣J
♠AK53          N          ♠10
♥K953                     ♥874
♦          W      E       ♦KJ86
♣AK982         S          ♣Q6543
            ♠QJ642
            ♥A62
            ♦1043
            ♣107
```

The bidding at the other table goes:

WEST	NORTH	EAST	SOUTH
1♣	2♦	3♣	Pass
6♣	All Pass		

The opposition make 920 against less pre-emptive bidding.

Of course the ace of hearts is in the South hand and the hearts break 3-3 making the slam a Pianola. Not exactly obvious, eh?

Possibly it would have been better for me as West to bid 4♦ instead of doubling with a void?

Anyway, 500 is better than making 420 in 5♣.

I have only included this next hand as it astounded me at the table, although I was grateful to the opposition. I was playing in a major summer tournament against a local and international team of Chinese speakers.

Dealer West, East-West Vulnerable

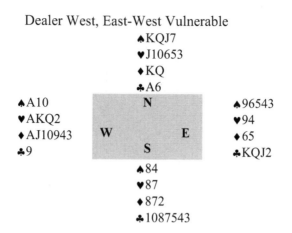

♠KQJ7
♥J10653
♦KQ
♣A6

♠A10
♥AKQ2
♦AJ10943
♣9

♠96543
♥94
♦65
♣KQJ2

♠84
♥87
♦872
♣1087543

The bidding:

WEST	NORTH	EAST	SOUTH
1♦	Double	1♠	Pass
2♥	Pass	2NT	Pass
3♦	3♥	Pass	4♣
Pass	Pass	Double	All Pass

As West I made a natural reverse showing strength and my two suits. Partner's 1♠ was natural 6+hcp and his 2NT was part of an agreement we have to show a limited strength hand.

My 3♦ showed I wanted to still get to game despite his limited response when suddenly North who had been fidgeting all along, suddenly bid 3♥. South looked very puzzled and emerged with his bid which my partner was happy to double.

Plus 800 points to the good guys led to a heated discussion by North-South all in Chinese with South pointing to my second bid.

I can only assume that North assumed because I had grey hair that I really didn't know what I was doing.
From a field of over 400 results, there was a range of 1100 plus to North-South to 800 plus East-West.

You have to learn that ageing gracefully (?) does have its advantages occasionally.

This next deal is a beauty. I am telling it from my partner's point of view. It was played in a major Pairs event in 8 graded sections comprising over 200 pairs. As West he held with Dealer North, Both Vulnerable:

♠KJ5
♥
♦1032
♣KQJ10432

North and East (me) passed and South opened 4♥. Partner bid 5♣. I later suggested that a pass would be a possibility, but he would have none of it and to be fair, a majority of the field also bid the same. North and East passed and South ventured 5♦, which North converted to 5♥. At our table, East (me) doubled and partner was on lead.

WEST	NORTH	EAST	SOUTH
	Pass	Pass	4♥
5♣	Pass	Pass	5♦
Pass	5♥	Double	All Pass

However, before you choose a lead, imagine a different scenario where over 5♥ I as East had bid 6♣ and South had bid 6♥ and then I as East had doubled.

So there are two questions. (a) What is your lead against 5♥X or (b) your lead against 6♥X.

Did you choose the safe K♣ for both questions? Well, have a look at what safety means.

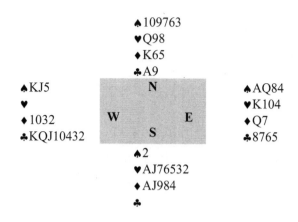

```
                    ♠109763
                    ♥Q98
                    ♦K65
                    ♣A9
      ♠KJ5              N              ♠AQ84
      ♥                                ♥K104
      ♦1032      W           E         ♦Q7
      ♣KQJ10432          S             ♣8765
                    ♠2
                    ♥AJ76532
                    ♦AJ984
                    ♣
```

The club lead not only provides a second entry to dummy, but also enables the spade pitch, allowing West to make thirteen tricks with a double hook of the hearts and the doubleton ♦Q falling.

A diamond lead will hold the hand to twelve tricks and a spade will hold it to eleven tricks. Our actual score was -1250, but this scored 27% whereas, had I pushed them to the small slam, it would have been -1860 and a complete zero.

Only one person in the whole field led a spade and one a diamond.

Some were in 5♣X either making or not but for a good score.

Passing the 5♥ bid would have resulted in -710 and resulted in a score above average. As I said, I would have passed West's hand.

Still it was Pairs which go hand in hand with lots of bidding. Partner and I were barely talking before this board, so you can imagine his demeanour after South claimed thirteen tricks.

Don't you just love this game?

Confucius says "When both pairs both play in the same strain, someone is wrong". This next deal is comical.

Dealer East, East-West Vulnerable

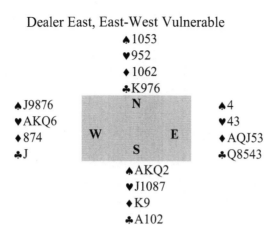

```
                    ♠1053
                    ♥952
                    ♦1062
                    ♣K976
   ♠J9876            N              ♠4
   ♥AKQ6                            ♥43
   ♦874       W          E          ♦AQJ53
   ♣J                S              ♣Q8543
                    ♠AKQ2
                    ♥J1087
                    ♦K9
                    ♣A102
```

Partner as East passes and South opens a 15-17hcp 1NT.

At this stage, I made what can only be described as a bad bid of 2♣ showing both majors. After North passes, my partner can save the board by bidding 2♦ which I will pass for a very good result, but he is not in a generous mood and picks his better major with a 2♥ bid. This trailed 2 off for minus 200.

At our partners' table, the bidding starts the same but West does not bid, leaving it to East to enter the fray. In a sequence that they wouldn't disclose, N-S end up in 4♥X which fortunately resulted only in a minus 300. Confucius knew what was going on – which is more than I can say for my team.

It's lead time again.

Dealer North, North-South Vulnerable

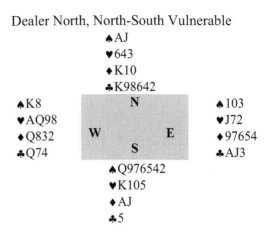

```
                    ♠AJ
                    ♥643
                    ♦K10
                    ♣K98642
    ♠K8              N              ♠103
    ♥AQ98                           ♥J72
    ♦Q832       W        E          ♦97654
    ♣Q74             S              ♣AJ3
                    ♠Q976542
                    ♥K105
                    ♦AJ
                    ♣5
```

North opened 1♣ and South bid 1♠. West (me) doubled and North bid
2♣. South bid 3♠ and North raised to 4♠.

WEST	NORTH	EAST	SOUTH
	1♣	Pass	1♠
Double	2♣	Pass	3♠
Pass	4♠	All Pass	

What do I lead? For reasons best known to me at the time, I led ♥A
which enabled declarer to wrap up ten tricks pretty quickly by the aid of
the spade situation.

The board was flat and my team mates were disappointed since the
hand records indicated that nine tricks was the limit of the hand.

While at lunch, I got a lecture from one of my team mates about how
aces are meant to beat kings. While chewing my sandwich I
temporarily felt guilty, but then thought about what would happen on a
minor suit lead (say a diamond).
South would win and lead his singleton club with the king losing to the
ace. If East returns a low heart, the ♥10 is played and West cannot
afford to play another heart as it sets up the tenth trick for declarer.
(The ♥J lead would be covered with the ♥K).

So a lead of a diamond or spade from West after winning one heart allows declarer to ruff clubs good by virtue of three entries to dummy (namely one diamond and two spades) resulting in eleven tricks. So cashing the second heart is best even though it doesn't defeat the contract.

At this point in time, I ascertained that a spade lead at trick one (any one will do) will defeat the contract (confirmed by Deep Finesse).

As I said earlier, this lead is only possible if it slipped from your grasp and became an exposed card. I previously thought bridge was already a hard game, but now I know it.

Two deals from the same night with something in common. The bidding goes South 1NT and North 3NT and it's your lead as West with the following:

♠Q7642
♥K973
♦Q4
♣85

Naturally you choose the ♠4 and now you see dummy:

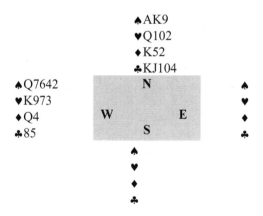

Declarer puts the ♠9 from dummy and then pauses for thought ending in his playing the ♠J and leading a low heart. Do you duck smoothly or not?

Ducking is good sometimes, but not tonight! Declarer wins the ♥10 and then rattles off nine tricks with a cackle.

The full hand:

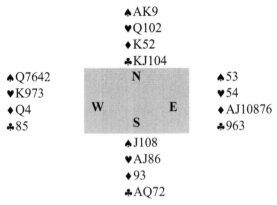

```
                    ♠AK9
                    ♥Q102
                    ♦K52
                    ♣KJ104
    ♠Q7642              N              ♠53
    ♥K973                               ♥54
    ♦Q4         W              E        ♦AJ10876
    ♣85                  S              ♣963
                    ♠J108
                    ♥AJ86
                    ♦93
                    ♣AQ72
```

Two chances to lead the ♦Q, but none taken. Only a difference of a few tricks and victory over defeat.

By now you will get the next lead right.

South opens 1♠ and North bids 2♥. South rebids 2♠ and North bids 3♣, which South raises to 4♣. North grimaces and bids 4♠. The whole auction is a bit tortured, but you as West are on lead again.

WEST	NORTH	EAST	SOUTH
			1♠
Pass	2♥	Pass	2♠
Pass	3♣	Pass	4♣
Pass	4♠	All Pass	

Deep Finesse demonstrates that the only card to beat the hand is the ♦Q. I know our West didn't think of that since he led a low diamond, but surely he should have been allowed to learn from his past experience, particularly an experience within the hour? The full hand:

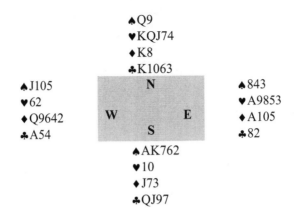

```
                        ♠Q9
                        ♥KQJ74
                        ♦K8
                        ♣K1063
    ♠J105               N               ♠843
    ♥62                                 ♥A9853
    ♦Q9642        W           E         ♦A105
    ♣A54                S               ♣82
                        ♠AK762
                        ♥10
                        ♦J73
                        ♣QJ97
```

The ♦Q forces declarer to play the ♦K (or he immediately loses four
fast tricks). After East wins with the ♦A, he switches to the ♣8 which
West ducks. The threat of a ruff forces declarer to draw trumps before
he can establish the hearts and retain an entry to dummy to use them.
A low diamond lead at trick one, ducked by declarer, allows declarer to
remain in control whatever the defence does.

It's weird that two hands should need the lead of the unsupported ♦Q
so close to each other.

It reminds me of the Robert Darvas book *Right Through the Pack* in
which he assigns importance and a story to each of the 52 cards
throughout his book.

On this night I guess it was the turn of the sparkling lady to feature.
Definitely worth an inclusion in the Exotica chapter, I surmise.

Another lead problem not involving the ♦Q.

South opens 1♥ and North bids 3♦ which is a Bergen Raise showing
four hearts and 10-11hcp. South raises to 4♥ after a little thought.

WEST	NORTH	EAST	SOUTH
			1♥
Pass	3♦	Pass	4♥
All Pass			

As West you are on lead again holding:

♠Q10532
♥A5
♦943
♣832

Have you decided?

Anyway, the full deal is:

```
                ♠64
                ♥QJ42
                ♦KQ105
                ♣J107
    ♠Q10532      N        ♠J987
    ♥A5                   ♥63
    ♦943      W     E     ♦A872
    ♣832         S        ♣AQ9
                ♠AK
                ♥K10987
                ♦J6
                ♣K654
```

Of course you lead any card from your outstanding club holding.

Declarer covers with the 10♣ and partner puts in the Q♣. Declarer must win the K♣ and when you win the A♥, a second club generates the setting trick.

It was so obvious I don't know why I bothered to ask.

Having nearly reached the end of this chapter, remember that obscure leads are only worth making if they lead to success, so don't make them too often unless you have asked yourself the Dirty Harry question

"Well Punk, do you feel lucky?"

The next deal has a bit of everything. Bad bidding, declarer play by the defence, lots of luck and a happy ending for the good guys which just qualifies it to be in this chapter.

The full deal is:

Dealer North, East-West Vulnerable

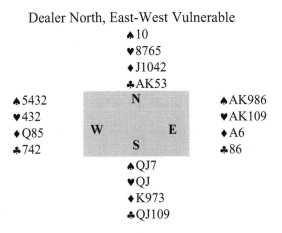

♠10
♥8765
♦J1042
♣AK53

♠5432   ♠AK986
♥432   ♥AK109
♦Q85   ♦A6
♣742   ♣86

♠QJ7
♥QJ
♦K973
♣QJ109

After North passed, partner East bid 1♠. South passed and it was my turn to bid. With only two points and a very flat shape the obvious bid is Pass.

However, I was enchanted by my low sequences (5432 and 432) and four spades so I decided to bid. We play Bergen raises, so the correct bid (assuming you have rejected Pass) is 3♠ showing four trumps and 0-6hcp. Partner may well pass this on a pessimistic day for a normal result.

However, a glance at the vulnerability and the other features of my hand made me a little nervous so I bid only 2♠ to "keep the bidding low". This bid showed at least 3-card support and 6-9hcp. This was the bad bidding component. Partner had an easy jump to 4♠ and South had an easy ♣Q lead.

Three rounds of clubs followed with partner ruffing the third. This was the defence assisting declarer part by completing the club elimination.

Partner played the ♠A,K revealing that South had a trump winner and followed up with ♥A,K picking up the ♥Q,J doubleton. He then stated that he would end-play South by either a heart ruff by South or otherwise by leading a spade lead and hoped that South held the ♦K which would secure the contract and plus 620. All of this came to pass which was the very lucky part.

Of course the contract can be defeated actively by North taking the second club and sending a diamond through or passively by North-South not playing a third club until later. I mention this as you might have thought that the result was a little unfair to North-South with the contract only being a very low single digit percentage chance.

The way I see it, my bad bidding gave them a chance to get a good score, but they didn't accept the gift.

Well, does this deal qualify as exotic? Perhaps I need a new chapter titled quixotic?

An environmentally friendly book printed and bound in England by www.printondemand-worldwide.com

PEFC Certified

This product is
from sustainably
managed forests
and controlled
sources

www.pefc.org

PEFC/16-33-415

MIX
Paper from
responsible sources
FSC® C004959

This book is made entirely of sustainable materials; FSC paper for the cover and PEFC paper for the text pages.

Reprint of # - C0 - 210/148/11 - CB - Lamination Gloss - Printed on 17-Dec-15 11:45